CIVIL WAR AND THE
INDIAN WARS

Indian youth play a hoop game to prepare for war.

CIVIL WAR AND THE INDIAN WARS

ROY BIRD
ILLUSTRATED BY MICHAEL ALMOND

PELICAN PUBLISHING COMPANY
GRETNA 2007

The word "Pelican" and the depiction of a pelican are trademarks
of Pelican Publishing Company, Inc., and are registered in the
U.S. Patent and Trademark Office.

Library of Congress Cataloging-in-Publication Data

Bird, Roy, 1952-
  Civil War and the Indian wars / by Roy Bird.
    p. cm.
  Includes bibliographical references and index.
  ISBN 978-1-58980-480-7 (pbk. : alk. paper) 1. Indians of North
America—Wars—1862-1865. 2. United States—History—Civil War,
1861-1865. 3. United States. Army. Cavalry—History—19th century.
I. Title.
  E83.863.B57 2007
  973.7—dc22   2007024935

Printed in the United States of America

Published by Pelican Publishing Company, Inc.
1000 Burmaster Street, Gretna, Louisiana 70053

For Laura

I've never given up on my dreams,
and neither should you.

Contents

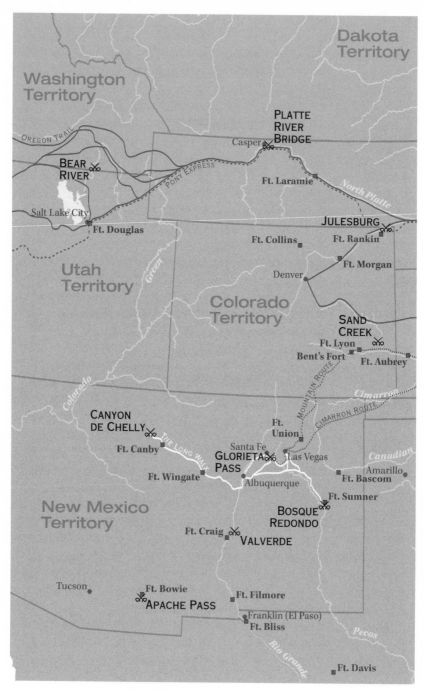

Map of Civil War and Indian Wars in the West.

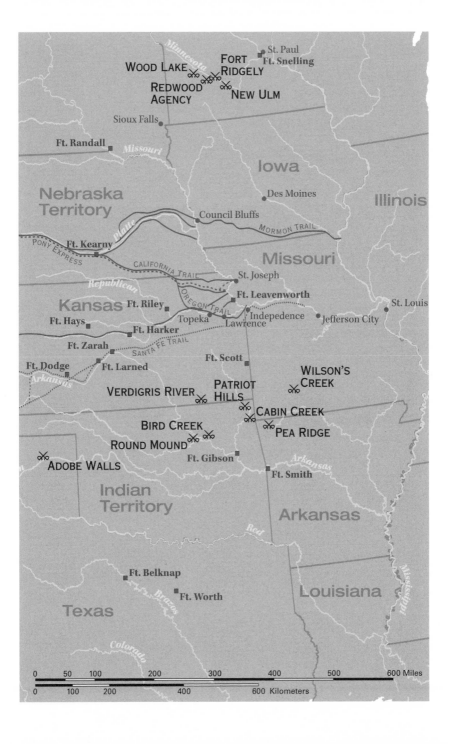

Preface

This account of some of the numerous conflicts between American Indians and whites during the American Civil War depicts the struggles between disenfranchised native peoples on the frontier and expansion of a predominantly white culture into the West. Even as whites fought whites from the Atlantic seaboard to the prairies of Kansas, great indigenous nations in places as far flung as Arizona, New Mexico, Utah, Montana, the Dakotas, Colorado, Nebraska, Kansas, Texas, Missouri, and Minnesota struck back at the incursion of the white intruders with their trappings of civilization and technology. This chronicle is based on events, incidents, and confrontations as they were recorded by contemporary writers and historians. Rather than breaking them into separate individual conflicts as so many historians have done, the intent of this volume is to treat all the Indian wars fought between 1861 and 1865 chronologically to examine the government's and the military's policies toward the "wild" American Indians of the West.

Most historians of the Indian wars seem to credit the War Between the States as a significant factor in the uprising of numerous tribes during these years. In fact, the continuous exposure to white civilization, the ongoing incursion by greedy whites with their modern technology, and an ambiguous government policy had caused frustration for the native peoples as much as two decades before the firing on Fort Sumter.

Neither condemnation nor justification for the Indian wars or the Civil War is the province of this book. The soldiers—in large part volunteers—were the instruments but often not the instigators of conquest. But frequently the officers in command were indeed bent on conquering the tribes they faced.

A writer of history must pay grateful tribute to his or her sources in the form of a bibliography and mention of repositories of material. Research for this book was chiefly accomplished in the State Library of Kansas, Mabee Library of Washburn University of Topeka, the Topeka and Shawnee County Public Library, and the Kansas State Historical Society. My own small collection of military and Western history books was useful.

Sincere thanks for generous and valued aid are offered to Michael Almond again for his fine artwork, and also to Darin Grauberger, Ryan Lash, and Emily Hadley of the University of Kansas Cartographic Service. I am indebted to Tom Schmiedeler for his advice and that of other members of the Washburn Center for Kansas Studies. And for the fifteenth time, this being my fifteenth book published, credit goes to my wife Luann for her patience with a husband who was present in the flesh but otherwise often gone to another time and place.

Introduction

Conflict between American Indians and whites dates back centuries to the arrival of the earliest European colonists. Native peoples often welcomed the new arrivals until the cavalier and colonizing attitudes of the immigrants stretched Indian patience to its limit. Both the Pilgrims in New England and settlers of Jamestown in Virginia soon saw fighting with the nearby tribes whose land they had usurped. The white people typically regarded Indians as uneducated savages at best, as subhuman and obstructions to progress at worst. They made the serious mistake of assuming that because the people they displaced were not as technologically advanced, they were less intelligent and inferior.

Conflicts continued and increased as the number of whites grew and spread west across the continent. People from both North and South moved west to exploit the vast richness of the Louisiana Territory in the first half of the nineteenth century. At first, the Indians west of the Mississippi River accepted these immigrants, but as their numbers grew and they despoiled the natural resources of the prairies, plains, and mountains that were home to the native peoples, friction increased.

The confrontations between individual tribes and the settlers simmered after the end of the Mexican War in 1848. Prior to that, various Indian groups such as the Apache and Navajo fought Mexicans and the Comanche fought Texans. The Republic of Texas became a state in 1845. In the treaty that ended the war with Mexico, that country turned over a mammoth swath of land in what are now the Southwest states that included the homelands of some of the Indians who had earlier raided Texans and Mexicans.

In Minnesota, similar actions by Indians were considered "uprisings." Along the Santa Fe, Smoky Hill, and Platte River trails, the warriors resorting to warfare were deemed "hostiles." In the mountains where gold, silver, and other mineral strikes occurred, the local tribes were barely tolerated briefly but then considered primitive impediments to the fortunes of greedy whites.

A little more than a decade of small raids and skirmishes on both sides led to total war in many cases. The conflicts might have continued on a minor level for much longer if not for the Civil War. Union soldiers left the western states and territories to battle Confederates, leaving a vacuum for the local tribes to step up raids. Also, in many cases the Regular Army officers were replaced by inept or intolerant volunteers who aggravated volatile situations.

Early in the war, Confederate troops from Texas tried to wrest control of the Southwest from the Federals. Confederate president Jefferson Davis dreamed of seizing the California gold fields through New Mexico and Arizona, controlling an area in which he had had an interest as U.S. secretary of war in the 1850s. But the South had to take over a large part of the country to fulfill this scheme. Although there was a small fight between Confederate and Union soldiers as far west as Picacho Pass on the stagecoach route in Arizona Territory, and the town of Tucson was occupied by a handful of Rebels for a brief time in February 1862, the South ultimately failed in this quest.

By 1863, with the Confederate forces routed back to Texas, the Federal government focused on the Indians. Until the arrival of white men, the enemies of most tribes had been other Indians. They had to rely on their own warriors to make war. They continued this style of warfare against white men. So the Federal troops were able to deal with each tribe on an individual basis, while the Indians fought piecemeal. The results were devastating for the tribes.

But it was not easy for the Federal government to overcome Indians while fighting Confederates elsewhere in the country. With regulars gone, state volunteers and local militia took their place. A large part of one whole regiment—the First New Mexico Volunteers—was of Mexican descent, traditional enemies of many Southwestern tribes. Another regiment, the Third Colorado Volunteers, was made up largely of merciless mountain miners. More than a few state volunteer soldiers found themselves facing Indians instead of the Rebels they had expected, and usually in primitive, unsettled, desolate parts of the country. Toward the end of the war, Confederate prisoners of war who volunteered to go west to fight Indians appeared on the frontier: the "Galvanized Yankees." Typically, both the state volunteer and the Galvanized Yankee regiments were stretched thin while trying to control the vastness of the American West.

The battle with American Indians had a direct effect on the War Between the States. They tapped important Federal manpower that might otherwise have been used against the Confederacy. They disrupted vital trade and communication routes. They slowed the progress of settlement and exploitation of the natural riches of the West.

At the same time, the battle with Indians had a direct impact on the Indian wars after the Civil War, on government Indian policies, and on the treatment of Indians in the future. Scorched-earth warfare was introduced to the Navajo, and annihilation was introduced to the Cheyenne and Arapaho at Sand Creek. A new concept of the reservation system was developed from the treatment of Apache and Navajo on the Bosque Redondo. Although the West remained part of the Union throughout the Civil War, the future of American Indians hinged on the outcome of the white men's struggle. When the Civil War ended, the American nation would turn its attention back to settling the West. The victors of the Civil War had little mercy on the defeated South, and they would have even less on the Indians in the West.

CIVIL WAR AND THE
INDIAN WARS

Mangas Coloradas.

CHAPTER 1

"The Fight Will Be Settled by White Men Without Indian Assistance": 1861

February 1861 suffered from a late-winter cold snap. The Butterfield stagecoach station employees at Apache Pass in the Mimbres Mountains of what would become southeastern Arizona Territory had run low on the firewood the local Chiricahua Apache had supplied since the depot was established in 1858. Ever since gold was discovered in 1860 near the old Spanish copper mines in the Mimbres, prospectors had flocked into the rocky, mountainous domain of Cochise, a tall, powerful, and dynamic leader of the Chiricahua Apache.

Until the gold rush to the teeming miners' camp at Pinos Altos, New Mexico Territory, and while other Apache raided on either side of the international boundary between Mexico and the United States, the Mimbres and Chiricahua made little trouble. Mangas Coloradas ("Red Sleeves") and his Mimbres followers permitted travelers to journey over the road from the Rio Grande River to Tucson in the southwestern corner of the New Mexico Territory that had been ceded to the United States after the Mexican War. The Chiricahua leader, Cochise, offered no opposition to the Butterfield stagecoaches that rolled along the southern route to California.

The tenuous peace came to an end when Mangas Coloradas and Cochise were personally attacked and insulted. In the autumn of 1860 Mangas Coloradas went among the many white gold seekers near Pinos Altos, the gold camp with nearly seven hundred miners by that time. The Apache people swore he went in his usual spirit of friendship—the white miners lamely claimed he tried to trick them into leaving the camp with the promise of gold elsewhere. Mangas Coloradas was seized, bound tightly to a tree, and scourged with the long supple goads used to drive oxen until his back was scarred with deep lacerations. For the proud Mimbres chieftain who had never been struck before, the humiliation made him a permanent enemy of the "White Eyes."

Even so, Cochise continued friendly relations with the whites until the cold February of the new year. A detachment of white soldiers of the Seventh U.S. Infantry under the command of Lt. George N. Bascom arrived in Apache Pass. The infantrymen pursued Apache who had raided east of the pass, allegedly stealing livestock and kidnapping a young boy of a frontier family. Bascom was new to the frontier and recognized no differences between Indians, even though his interpreter was fluent in several Apache dialects. The lieutenant, supported by about sixty men, powwowed with Cochise, the Chiricahua Apache chieftain best known to the white soldiers.

At the parley, Cochise explained that Coyotero Apache had committed the raid, not his own Chiricahua. In the soldier chief's tent, Bascom would not believe Cochise, and he demanded that the Apache leader surrender the white boy. When Cochise explained that he could not for the simple reason that his people did not hold the lad, the lieutenant assumed that the chief refused to free the boy. At last, his patience exhausted, Bascom ordered Cochise arrested. When soldiers tried to hold Cochise hostage in the tent, the huge chief drew a knife in an indignant rage at the white men's treachery, slashed his way through the canvas wall, and sprinted away amid a flurry of musket balls. Five members of Cochise's relatives were not so fortunate, nor so agile. Other soldiers seized them as hostages as they waited outside the tent. Moving along the road through Apache Pass, Cochise and his warriors seized a Butterfield station employee and two travelers to exchange for his relatives. Bascom adamantly refused. Cochise struck back, massacring drovers of a train of freight wagons plodding along behind ox teams through the pass, tried to dry gulch a Butterfield stagecoach, and suddenly attacked white soldiers watering stock at Apache Springs. The stubborn Bascom found himself besieged and dispatched a courier to the nearest fort with an urgent call for help.

The messenger reported a number of wounded, so Asst. Surgeon John Dowling (or Bernard J.) Irwin volunteered to lead the reinforcement of about fourteen volunteers. Mounted on mules, they rode through a blinding snowstorm toward the plains at the mouth of the pass where Bascom's force desperately held out. Irwin led his intrepid little command in an attack that surprised the Chiricahua, intent on pressing Bascom, in an onslaught that routed the red warriors. Surgeon Irwin immediately dismounted, removed the instruments he had been able to carry in the medical kit in his saddle bags on his mule, and treated the wounded.

Cochise's village was found and destroyed by troops with Irwin in tow. But after the weeklong standoff, Cochise cut and ran to Mexico. Beside the road through the pass the white hostages he had taken were left terribly mutilated. In turn, the white men hanged Cochise's relatives from a tree, in clear sight of the road, where their corpses swung in the wind for months afterward. Although the Congressional Medal of Honor had not been created yet, Irwin was awarded it retroactively in 1894 for his distinguished gallantry during the engagement with the Chiricahua near Apache Pass. Irwin eventually rose to the rank of brigadier general, chief medical officer of the United States Army, and post surgeon at Fort Riley, Kansas, from 1866 to 1867 and again from 1871 to 1873. The Irwin Army Hospital at Fort Riley today is named for him.

The spring of 1861 saw the renewal of Indian attacks on settlers' cabins and Pony Express stations. As soon as the grass was green enough to support ponies, minor hostilities erupted.

The frontier simmered as tribesmen raided on their own account or took sides with either the Confederacy or the Union in the developing Civil War.

From the moment that Fort Sumter was fired upon, it was clear the Indians would take part in the conflict. Indians from many parts of the continent took interest in the war between the whites. Among them was a remarkable Seneca sachem, Ely Samuel Parker. To further not only himself but also his people, Parker had studied law, but the United States Supreme Court denied all Indians admission to the bar because they were not American citizens. Parker then pursued an education in civil engineering at Rensselaer Polytechnic Institute. And before the war he formed a friendship with former Army captain Ulysses S. Grant on a construction project near Galena, Illinois.

At the outset of the Civil War between the white men, Parker attempted to enlist in the regular U.S. Army to which Grant had returned. He was rudely refused a commission by Secretary of War William Seward. That fight, wrote the Secretary, would be settled by white men without any Indian assistance—a proclamation that would be flatly contradicted repeatedly during the next five years. Parker at last wrangled a captaincy in the Army Corps of Engineers, and he would eventually recruit 628 Iroquois volunteers.

While Parker endeavored to enlist, it was clear that the tribes removed from the South during the Jacksonian era and settled arbitrarily in the Indian Territory (modern Oklahoma) would also be drawn into the war. Many of these people were from the South and owned slaves, had adopted plenty of the white lifestyles of the Southerners, and more than a few felt an affinity for Southerners. Added to that was the fact that a good share of their agents were from the seceding states. The geographical proximity of Indian Territory to Arkansas and Texas, both states that had seceded, made it easier for agents of the South to sway members of the Five Civilized Tribes to the Confederate cause. The Chickasaw and the Choctaw committed overwhelmingly to the South. The Seminoles, Creeks, and Cherokees split their loyalties.

The influence of trusted Indian agents, mostly Southerners, counted largely. Albert Pike, a poet and politician from Arkansas, crossed the border to enter the Territory as a Confederate Indian commissioner with the responsibilities of arranging treaties allying the Five Civilized Tribes with the Confederacy and enlisting Indians into regiments to supplement the South's Trans-Mississippi West military organizations. Ironically, Pike offered the transplanted tribes more liberal treaties that the United States had ever offered. Some signed the treaties quite readily, while others tried to remain neutral in the forthcoming war.

Among the Cherokee, John Ross, an old and respected leader from the days in North Carolina and Tennessee, spoke eloquently in an attempt to keep his people out of the white men's fight: "I am—the Cherokee are—your friends," he said to Confederate sympathizers who came to the Cherokee Nation, "but we do not wish to be brought into the feuds between yourselves and your Northern Brethren. Our wish is for peace. Peace at home and Peace among you." Ross had seen the Cherokee torn asunder by removal by Andrew Jackson's administrative policy in the "Trail of Tears" of the 1830s. Factions formed at the time the Cherokee were expelled from North Carolina, Georgia, and Tennessee divided them again, and the Creeks as well, between North and South. Those who opposed the removal threw their support behind Ross's rivals, whose supreme chief was Stand Watie. Not only did Stand Watie advocate joining the Confederacy, he also recruited the best Cherokee regiment to serve the South.

Pike seemed successful in carrying the majority of the Five Tribes for the Confederacy, promising large monetary subsidies and gifts such as Rebel flags. He was also allegedly successful at rousing the Kiowa and Comanche to attack Union wagon trains along the Santa Fe Trail. However, if Pike indeed roused those tribes of the Southern Plains, his job was made infinitely easier because of the general attitude of whites on the frontier. Certainly, Pike communicated with the Comanche

Stand Watie.

and Kiowa, as did other Southerners plotting to disrupt communication and trade along the Santa Fe Trail. It served not only as a supply route to keep food and fodder flowing out to the forts in New Mexico Territory, which still included what is now Arizona, but also was the southern link with resources in the state of California. Cutting this slender lifeline could give the Confederacy vital control of the crucial American West.

The increased traffic on the Santa Fe Trail caused another military problem for the Union. The Comanche and Kiowa, Arapaho and Southern Cheyenne, resented the almost constant incursions into their lands, and tension ran high on the High Plains during the summer of 1861. The Unionists who crossed the Great Plains considered the tribesmen at best inferior, at worst aborigines interfering with progress and fomenting hostilities deserving extermination. In mining camps, at trading posts, and at stagecoach stations from Kansas to California the Southern Plains tribes were insulted, humiliated, physically abused, and sometimes outright attacked. The Indians quite naturally returned the treatment in kind, so whites at those places lived in fear of most red men.

Further north, in Kansas—only a state for a few months at that time—and in Nebraska Territory the Arapaho and Southern Cheyenne and Sioux were equally ill-treated by brash, boorish, and cavalier freighters, gold seekers, and other travelers on the Smoky Hill and Platte River roads. Incursions into their hunting grounds had begun much earlier with fur trappers, followed by immigrants on the Oregon and California Trails with whom clashes were inevitable. Especially around Denver, Indian baiting had developed into a fine art.

Before 1861, Kansas Territory stretched west all the way to the peaks of the Rocky Mountains. The area included much of the Front Range—indeed, the very name of Denver City came from a governor of Kansas Territory. In 1859, when gold was discovered at Cherry Creek, Denver City sprouted almost overnight. The Fifty-niners, as participants in this gold rush were called, filled the area and increased traffic on the Platte

River Road many times over. The miners spilled over, too, heading southwest to Apacheria at Pinos Altos. At both mining areas, Indians were treated not only with disdain but even with violence and brutality.

Denver grew quickly until 1861. The boomtown was served by three routes—the northern trail along the Platte River to Julesburg, Colorado Territory; the southern route along the Santa Fe Trail past the Big Timbers on the Arkansas River to Bent's Fort, then north along the east slope of the Rockies; and the central trail through Kansas along the Smoky Hill River. The gold rush attracted plenty of well-intentioned fortune seekers but also some mighty unsavory characters, and they came from both the North and the South. During the spring of 1861, Denver witnessed confrontations between Union men and Southern sympathizers. The only common characteristic between the two white factions was hatred of the Indians.

The threat by these whites brought retaliation. After April 1861, the Sioux along the Platte River in Nebraska and the Southern Cheyenne and Arapaho along the Smoky Hill River and the Santa Fe Trail in Kansas took natural advantage of the Civil War's drain on white manpower. They raided far and wide. By the summer, troops were spread thin to protect the trails and the tiny settlements. However, most of these were to a large extent retaliatory raids, small isolated incidents that were typical of the Indian style of warfare. Unlike the first major battle between whites at Manassas, Virginia, in July 1861, the Plains Indians could rarely be brought to bay in pitched battle.

Still further north the Santee, or Eastern Sioux, on a long, narrow reservation in Minnesota also watched as the white men in the state enlisted in regiments to defend the Union. With the outbreak of the War Between the States, the attention of the white population focused less on the farming, railroad building, and town development occupations that built the state and the pacification of the Santee Sioux that made them possible, and more on preserving the Union that Minnesota had joined only a few years earlier.

The Santee—known colloquially by some whites as the "farmer Sioux"—had been in contact with whites for generations. Fort St. Anthony (later Fort Snelling) was established by Zebulon Pike at the confluence of the Minnesota and Mississippi Rivers in 1819, and it became the center of early white settlement. Henry Hastings Sibley established the headquarters of the American Fur Company in 1834 at Mendota, across the river from the fort. For two decades afterward great trains of ox carts carried bales of furs from the Red River Valley in the north and the Dakota plains to the west, and the Santee Sioux in close proximity to Sibley's trading post. Just north of the post a community that came to be known as St. Paul grew so rapidly as virgin prairie was preempted for farmland that it became the territorial capital in 1849.

The white population of the Minnesota Territory by 1850 was a mere 6,000, but a treaty with the Santee Sioux the next year opened up the fertile western prairies of the state to white settlement while restricting the Sioux to a small reservation. By 1857 there were more than 150,000 settlers, and Minnesota was admitted to the Union as a free state in 1858.

Military support of the Union in 1861 drained the state of young men of military age as well as Federal troops which left Minnesota unprotected against the Sioux, many of whom resented the cession of their lands. The treaty between the Santee and the United States government promised an annual distribution of annuities. These came partly in the form of food and trade goods, partly in cash.

The leading chief, Little Crow, had been instrumental in convincing the Santee to agree to the treaty that squeezed his people into a ten-mile-wide reserve reaching 150 miles up and down the western Minnesota River. Little Crow watched with the other Sioux as the whites became caught up in their own warfare, for the first time in a decade ignoring his people in the excitement of saving the Union. Despite his oratorical skill and persuasive power, many of the more dissatisfied Santee regarded him as a tool of the whites. All the Sioux observed that after the fight in Virginia in July the annuities were slow to come in July and August 1861. Reservation life was not pleasant, with Little Crow's followers cutting their hair, moving into square log houses, and trying to farm in the white man's way. Fewer and fewer of the promised annuities made their way to the Indians; the goods wound up in merchants' warehouses, as the money due to the Indians wended its way into corrupt officials' pockets, including those of fur trader Sibley, who went on to become the state's first governor.

A similar volatile situation existed for different reasons in the Southwest. The arrival of the Civil War intensified the deteriorating relationships the Navajo had with each other as well as with the Mexican population of New Mexico Territory. Navajo and Mexicans had led an ambiguous existence, alternately raiding and counterraiding then carrying out *congenial* trade and barter. In 1861 as the frontier regulars of the United States Army were called to battlefields in the East, New Mexicans—many of them of Mexican heritage—joined the First New Mexico Volunteers and garrisoned the forts and towns against the hostile Navajo.

Adding to the explosive mixture, the Navajo themselves were generally either *ladrones* or *ricos*. *Ladrones* were poor in numbers of sheep and possessions, while the *ricos* measured their wealth and prosperity by the size of their flocks and herds. Those who took part in raiding usually were *ladrones* seeking to improve their personal circumstances by looting Mexican settlers. The Mexicans sought revenge by falling upon the more pastoral *ricos* who were more sedentary and who appeared to be the perpetrators because their flocks increased. The peaceably disposed *ricos* lost sheep, horses, crops, and prestige. During the 1850s, raids by Mexicans, American military activity, and friction with the growing white population all increased. *Ricos* became identified among fellow Navajo as the peace party friendly to whites, but the *ladrones* grew ever more warlike. As *ricos* became impoverished by the Mexican raids and the acts of unscrupulous traders, the ranks of the *ladrones* who were hostile increased as those desiring peace diminished.

By 1861 the Navajo joined other tribes throughout the American West as they watched bluecoats depart for the war between white men in the East. They also watched their Apache neighbors to the west in violent confrontation with "White Eyes." Word of the conflict of the Mimbres of Mangas Coloradas and the fights of Cochise's Chiricahua, passed through the Coyotero and Mescalero Apache who were next door to the Navajo. Albert Pike may have been stirring up the Kiowa and Comanche who bordered the Navajo on the east, while the Confederates in Texas cast covetous eyes on New Mexico and its jewel, Santa Fe.

The summer of 1861 was one of tense observation, watchful waiting, throughout the frontier territories. Thousands of American Indians from the deserts of New Mexico Territory to the high plains of Texas, Kansas, and Nebraska, from the Rocky Mountains to the prairie near the Great Lakes, paid close attention to the white men's activities as the frontier became secondary in the national consciousness. To the Indians, a war between different factions of whites made sense, for among most of them war was a series of small raids and personal bravery. They could not conceive a war on the scale that was coming—of course, neither could the whites of North and South among whom the war fomented.

Word of the great battle far away in midsummer trickled to the tribes, mostly from the whites still on the frontier. The Indians saw many of the whites who had pressured them leave to go back from whence they had come, and the Southern whites had apparently won the big fight. But soon word came of another Southern victory, this one at Wilson's Creek in Missouri, which was much closer to many of the tribes. It also had greater impact on the Indians.

Some of the Indians who had had less contact with civilization assumed that a new day had dawned. And whites, too, thought the frontier settlements and the thin travel routes lay perilously exposed to the Indian threat. Both the Federal government and the Confederate authorities mobilized for war against each other, and both determined to allow volunteers on their western borders to deal with the tribesmen. The Indians assumed that they now had an opportunity to drive whites from the West, who in many cases had expanded their footholds with new silver and gold discoveries in the Nevada Territory, Idaho Territory, Oregon, and Montana Territory in 1860 and 1861.

The Indians who knew white people better recognized that resistance would be temporary at best. In 1861, Colorado, Nevada, and Dakota Territories were created. The state of California had been linked with the rest of the United States by a single thread of communication since April 1860. News was relayed by messengers on horseback. Only nine days before Fort Sumter, on April 3, 1861, the Pony Express celebrated its first—and only—anniversary. It would go out of business in October 1861, when the telegraph sped communication between California and the Union. This development would impact the Indians more than they would ever know.

Indians were not the Confederates' only interest in the West. Certainly, Indian hostilities would draw off Yankee resources and manpower. Yet Southerners were as ambitious about Western expansion and exploitation of natural resources as their Northern counterparts. With early victories and Union desperation, it seemed that the territories of the Southwest, the gold and silver mines being opened, even California itself, were within the grasp of the South.

The war came to the West in July 1861 when Lt. Col. John Robert Baylor, in command of a battalion of the Confederate Second Texas Mounted Volunteers, occupied Fort Bliss, Texas, at Franklin, now El Paso. The post had been abandoned by Union troops on March 31. Fort Bliss became the launching point for Southern operations in the Southwest. An early Rebel influence on the frontier, Henry Hopkins Sibley (no relation to the Minnesota Sibley), a United States Army major, had resigned his commission in May and passed Fort Filmore, the southernmost New Mexico post still occupied by Federal troops. He proclaimed that he was now "the enemy" and would return soon. Then he rode the forty miles down the Rio Grande River Valley to Fort Bliss to begin organizing an invasion force.

Near Fort Filmore on the west bank of the Rio Grande lay the small town of La Mesilla, already a hotbed of Southern sympathies—indeed, the Stars and Bars already flew over the town, and there was little the Union soldiers in the fort could do about it. Sibley organized a brigade of Texas volunteers of 2,500 mounted men with the Second Texas at its core to march first to Fort Filmore, then advance to Santa Fe to control the terminus of the Santa Fe Trail. One source says that in addition to that part of his mission, Sibley "determined, as good policy, to encourage private enterprise against the Navajo and Apache Indians by legalizing the enslaving of them."

To defend against the Rebel threat, the Union could muster forces from two sources. One was out in California. Early in 1861 there had been secessionist activity, especially in the southern part of the state where the southern route of the Butterfield Overland Express terminated. These Southern sympathizers were quelled by California volunteers from the northern reaches of the state led by a steely man, James Carleton. Carleton's Californians might be sent east on the southern route if the Confederates moved across the New Mexico Territory toward their state or tried to threaten the silver works in Nevada Territory.

The other Union force on the frontier was in Colorado Territory. In Denver and the mining camps strung like pearls along the Front Range, Southerners represented about a third of the population, with the militant ones known as "bummers." Late in April 1861, the bummers, led by Arkansas native and pistoleer Charley Harrison, took a stab at gaining control over the territory. Members of the First Colorado Volunteer Infantry Regiment drubbed the secessionists, driving them underground by sheer weight of numbers. The Colorado volunteers represented a force that could move south into New

Mexico Territory or east onto the plains of Kansas in the cases that Confederates attempted to seize Santa Fe or that bummers plotted to disrupt communication and trade on the Santa Fe Trail, two-thirds of which crossed Kansas.

Both the Californians and the Coloradans would see as much action against Indian enemies as those in gray. Yet for the time being the South appeared to have made the most progress toward securing the cooperation or collaboration or at least acquiescence of the Indians on the frontier. Albert Pike and Confederate agents like him secured Indians for the South by promising money, gifts, and even rights and privileges for which the Five Civilized Tribes had vainly sought for a half-century. Could such promises be kept?

It certainly seemed so when news of the Confederate victory at Manassas in July 1861, followed by the lesser but more important one for the Indians of the Five Tribes (because it was near at hand and because a small number of warriors from Indian Territory served in Arkansas regiments) bore witness to the prowess of Southern arms at Wilson's Creek in Missouri on August 10, 1861.

A formal vote of secession was passed by the Cherokee Nation council in August 1861, and there was nothing to imply that the secession ordinance would fail to bind the entire tribe. In fact the only opposition among any of the Five Tribes in the Territory was on the part of an octogenarian minor chief of the Creek Nation named Opothleyoholo.

When Col. Douglas Cooper, once a trusted agent to the Choctaw but by then a Confederate officer, arrived in the Creek Nation of Indian Territory, he found as many as six thousand pro-Union Creek, a few Seminole, and a few African-Americans who had escaped from slavery and fled to the Nations. Those people gathered around old Opothleyoholo's home, and small bands of his pro-Union followers clashed with scouts of pro-Confederate Creek leaders Daniel and Chilly McIntosh.

Faced with a choice between submitting to the Confederate

tribes or fighting his way out, Opothleyoholo did not hesitate. He marched toward Union Kansas in November 1861. The old Creek chief had been promised by a United States Indian agent in Kansas that the Federal troops there would soon cross from his state into the Nations and help the loyal Indians drive the Rebels out. Even so, Opothleyoholo moved his multitude numbering almost 4,000 people—1,700 warriors and the rest women, children, and aged—along with the tribal treasury and a large amount of livestock. By November 15, 1861, Colonel Cooper had marshaled a force of 1,400 Rebel soldiers—900 Indians from the First Choctaw and Chickasaw Mounted Rifles, the First Seminole Cavalry Battalion, and the First Creek Cavalry along with 500 white volunteers of the Ninth Texas Cavalry. Neither the Union nor the Confederate Indians were well-armed or well-clothed. Their weapons ranged from rifled muskets to smoothbores and old, almost useless flintlocks and a small number of old revolvers dating to the 1830s and 1840s. A few on either side were reduced to fighting with bows and arrows. Uniforms were nonexistent, and civilian clothing was mostly nondescript.

The men of the Ninth Texas Cavalry pursued some of the Union Creek at about 4:00 P.M. on November 19, 1861, only to learn as so many white men would that they were really only decoys. As darkness rapidly approached, the Creek decoys led the gullible Texans to a tree-lined stream near some high ground known as Round Mound. The wily Opothleyoholo sprang his trap. Twice the old chief and his Creek warriors fended off their Rebel attackers. On the third attempt Confederate Indians joined the fray, charging the pro-Union camp over icy ground. Creek small arms fire toppled riders from their slipping, sliding mounts. Then the Union Creek set fire to the dry grass of the late autumn prairie to cover their withdrawal after the battered Rebel ranks beat a hasty disorganized retreat. When they warily advanced on the Round Mound battlefield the next morning, they found Opothleyoholo's encampment empty.

The renewed pursuit lasted for ten days before the Confederates caught up and brought on another engagement. Colonel Cooper tried to envelop the retreating Creek between two columns. But confusion ensued, and at Opothleyoholo's camp on Bird Creek, the same determined resistance and the fact that Col. John Drew's First Cherokee Mounted Rifles regiment of secessionists declined to fight fellow Indians who were victims of an unjust and relentless pursuit, harmed the effectiveness of the Confederate army. The Battle of Bird Creek was one more fought on Opothleyoholo's terms on December 9, 1861. The Union Indian fighters held off the remaining enemies for about four hours. Colonel Cooper finally ceased his pursuit and withdrew. Fearing that his defeats at Round Mound and Bird Creek and the desertion of Colonel Drew's First Cherokee might shift the Indian Territory loyalties from the South to the Union, Cooper called to the neighboring Confederate state of Arkansas for help. A column of almost 1,600 Arkansas and Texas cavalry including veterans of Wilson's Creek responded. Also supporting Cooper was Col. Stand Watie and his Second Cherokee Mounted Rifles. None of these reinforcements would fall for any of the Creek tricks. They caught up with and punished the Union Indians severely at the Battle of Patriot Hills. In the running fight many of the pro-Union Creek warriors were killed or wounded, noncombatants were captured, and livestock and supplies seized as booty.

This was more than the weakening Creek could bear. They lost almost seven hundred dead in three battles and to starvation and exposure. Once they finally crossed the border into Kansas, they were protected from the secessionist harassment, but while they were safe under the protection of Kansas volunteer regiments they were utterly and completely miserable. Relegated to the reservations of other tribes, mostly from the old Northwest Territory states of Ohio, Indiana, and Illinois, the destitute refugees suffered terribly through the exceptionally severe winter of 1861–62. Efforts of authorities to provide for them were limited because of bickering between Kansas

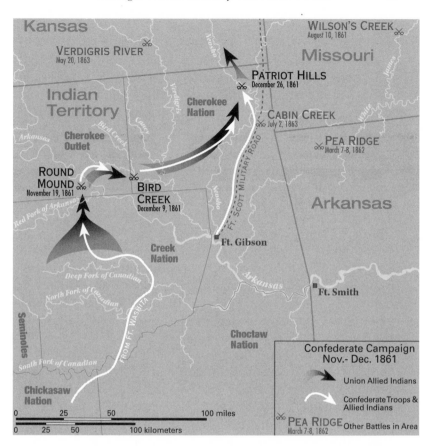

and Federal officials about where responsibility for the refugees lay. Failing supplies, inadequate from the start, blistering cold, and rapidly spreading disease made it essential for the loyal Creek, the Seminole and African-Americans with them, and the men from among the First Cherokee regiment's deserters who fled north, be helped back to the Indian Territory before another winter set in.

As 1861 drew to an unusually cold close, American Indians from the lakes of Minnesota to the sands of New Mexico Territory, from the banks of the Mississippi River to the peaks of the Western mountains were aware of the big fight among the white men. Some, like the Chiricahua and Mimbres Apache, had already seen violent conflict with whites that would soon burst into open warfare. Others, like the Navajo and the Santee Sioux, smoldered with discontent and suffered outrages that could have easily been avoided, even as militant bands fostered ill will toward whites. Still others actually took up arms for one side or the other in the white man's war, as did the Five Civilized Tribes of the Indian Territory. Regardless of the stance that different people took toward the Civil War in the East, hindsight demonstrates that the American Indians would be impacted by the continent-wide conflagration.

Both the North and the South curried the favor of American Indians. The Confederacy did more to enlist the aid of Indians in the fight in Indian Territory by encouraging actual secession of the Five Tribes and recruiting battalions and regiments to supplement Southern manpower. Among the Plains Indians, Rebel agents may have incited warriors to disrupt Union travel and communication with the vital resources of the West. Yet the Confederates from the frontier, on the other hand, held the same low opinion of all Indians and felt no compunction about exterminating them or reducing them to slavery as Sibley planned.

Northerners did not outwardly seek out the aid of Indians— in fact, they actually rejected it. But the Indian policy, never particularly humane or strong, became ludicrous as attention focused ever heavily on the struggle to preserve the Union. The Yankee government continued to view the Indian frontier as an obstacle to progress, civilization, and America's destiny. Although occasionally the Federals opened their arms to Indians—case in point, the fugitive Creek, Seminole, and mutinied Cherokee in Kansas—such hesitant benevolence was typically tempered by bureaucratic bumbling and Westerners' inherent dislike and distrust of the Indians.

Mangas Coloradas and his Mimbres were holed up in their mountains at the end of the first year of the Civil War. Cochise and his Chiricahua had fled to Mexico and bided their time before returning with a vengenance. Ely Samuel Parker, the full-blood Seneca, sought a commission in the Union Army, and pro-Confederate leaders of the Five Tribes recruited regiments to fight for the South. Rebel agents may have tried to get the Plains tribes to raid along trails and attack outposts—Unionists were thoroughly convinced that such chicanery happened—and even if no Southerners encouraged them, the policies and attitudes of the whites in the West generated more than enough animosity. Both the Santee Sioux in the north under Little Crow and the Navajo in the south led by *ladrones* were pressed to the breaking point by dishonest traders and agents, by poor treatment from settlers and miners, and by outright raiding. The Confederates in Texas ambitiously cast avaricious eyes toward the west and northwest, even as Yankee soldiers abandoned or turned over military posts, returned to the great struggle in "the States," and allowed volunteers to fill the stations remaining in Federal hands.

The end of the first year of the Civil War found American Indians still in weary watch-and-wait circumstances. Some thought the time was ripe to strike at the white intruders; some felt desperation or righteous indignation that would turn them hostile; some believed their futures were hitched to the wagons either of the Union or the Confederacy. The watch-and-wait situation would change dramatically in the coming year as the frontier exploded at innumerable, inevitable flash points.

Col. Kit Carson.

CHAPTER 2

"Let Them Eat Grass": 1862

Robert Edward R. S. Canby was a tall, silent, intelligent, and industrious Kentuckian who had been appointed commander of the District of New Mexico in May 1861, succeeding Col. William Loring of North Carolina. Loring resigned his Federal commission and extended his service to the Confederacy after the failure of his plot to turn everything under his control to the South. Upon assuming command of the District of New Mexico because he was one of the few loyal senior officers left in the Territory, Colonel Canby had his hands full. That May he had Indian wars brewing on his doorstep at the same time he intercepted a letter from Maj. Henry Hopkins Sibley, now at Fort Bliss wearing Confederate gray. Sibley urged other Federal officers in New Mexico Territory to defect to the Confederacy. Canby immediately sent instructions for Sibley's arrest as a traitor, but he had already reached the safety of seceded Texas. Ironically, Canby and Sibley were related by marriage—their wives were distant cousins.

A great deal depended on Colonel Canby. His troops suffered poor morale and had not been paid in months. Most of them now looked forward to going east to more active theaters of war—at least maybe there they would get paid. Canby lacked sufficient troops to garrison the military posts that had not been abandoned by the Federals. Supplies were limited, and no one knew when more would arrive along the six hundred miles of the Santa Fe Trail through the stricture of the Plains Indian raiders. The colonel had little faith in the local New Mexicans as volunteers or militia.

Canby struggled with a surfeit of secessionists and a scarcity of Unionists. But the withdrawal of soldiers inspired Mimbres and Chiricahua to lash back at the whites again. Travelers and settlers alike suffered. The mining town of Pinos Altos was the victim of a direct attack by Apache, followed by a siege that caused most of the miners to light out for more secure surroundings. A small detachment of Confederate soldiers that crossed the desert to occupy Tucson made no attempt to defend the town. The Apache warriors carefully dodged the "Arizona Rangers"—vigilantes drawn from among the miners purportedly for self-defense but clearly riding the vengeance trail.

Early in 1862, Canby's full attention centered on Rebels. Henry Hopkins Sibley prepared to make good on his promise to return to New Mexico Territory. Canby found himself at Fort Marcy, New Mexico Territory, with Mimbres in the hills and Confederates at Fort Filmore and the town of La Mesilla. Louisianan Sibley—inventor of the Sibley tent designed along the lines of Plains Indian tepees and the Sibley stove to accompany it—now held the rank of brigadier general in the Confederate Army. He raised his brigade of the Fourth, Fifth, and Seventh Texas Volunteer regiments—including two companies of lancers—and a small battery of howitzers. Col. John R. Baylor and his Second Texas Mounted Rifles had already established the Confederate Territory of Arizona south of the 34th Parallel. The planned Rebel conquest of the Southwest had begun.

Fort Craig was the only Federal bastion in the way of the Confederate invasion. It was becoming a sprawling military base commanded by Maj. Thomas Duncan and part of his Third U.S. Cavalry. The Third had been the Regiment of Mounted Rifles since its creation in 1846. It had been redesignated in August 1861, when the First and Second Regiments of

Dragoons had been renamed the First and Second Cavalry while the original First and Second Cavalry were renumbered to the Fourth and Fifth U.S. Cavalry. The Fort Craig garrison also included units of the Second and Fifth Cavalry, the Fifth and Seventh Infantry, some Colorado volunteers, and a battery of six bronze smoothbore cannon. Nearby were up to several thousand Union recruits and militia. Col. Benjamin S. Roberts, Third Cavalry, was now the colonel of the Fifth New Mexico Volunteer Infantry regiment and commander of the southern military district of New Mexico Territory with headquarters at Fort Craig.

On the morning of February 21, 1862, those two forces clashed at Valverde—the Green Valley—across the Rio Grande River and seven miles north from Fort Craig. The Texas horse soldiers charged the Union forces in an attempt to capture one or more of the four fords, command of which would open the way to capture the fort. Fighting dismounted, Yankee cavalrymen and a couple of the old howitzers fended off mounted charges, then at midmorning settled down to a rifle and artillery duel as Sibley tried to flank the right of the Federal position by extending his lines farther down the river to another ford. Colonel Roberts was hard pressed until reinforcements arrived in the form of the First New Mexico Volunteers under the legendary Col. Christopher "Kit" Carson. He and his men took position on the west bank near the Valverde Road. The artillery exchange continued throughout the afternoon with storming thrusts by both bluecoats and Texans. Then, as dusk approached, a determined Confederate assault captured the Union battery. The guns were turned on the fleeing Federals as they fell back to positions near the fort. Among the Union dead at the Battle of Valverde was George Bascom, Seventh U.S. Infantry, who had caused so much trouble among the Apache a year earlier.

Valverde was a tactical victory for the Confederates, but a costly one. Sibley captured Albuquerque and advanced north toward Santa Fe and Colonel Canby's headquarters at Fort Marcy. The Fourth Texas was reduced to a large battalion of foot soldiers because they had lost so many horses at Valverde. Then in March the weather turned bitterly cold as Sibley threatened Santa Fe. His column with a supply train of about seventy wagons moved through the mountainous terrain, arriving at Glorieta Pass.

Maj. John M. Chivington, a frontier clergyman with political ambitions, led four companies of the First Colorado Volunteers, two companies of the Fifth U.S. Infantry, and James Ford's Independent Company of Colorado Volunteers as they split away from the main Union column on March 28, 1862, to strike the exhausted men and teams of the invaders. As the freezing sun settled in the afternoon, four hundred men charged the supply train. That morning the Rebels attacked the rest of the Union column at the mouth of Glorieta Pass at a place called Pigeon's Ranch. The outnumbered bluecoats were forced to retire, but not before the Rebel supply wagons attacked by Chivington and his men were burned, the Rebel horses and mules killed, and the Rebels had won another Pyrrhic victory. Sibley and his 1,800 remaining men were driven out after the supply train's destruction.

The Indians of the Great Plains and the Southwest were guaranteed after Valverde and Glorieta Pass that they could only confront bluecoat white men. On the other hand, two of those were the inimitable Kit Carson and the "fighting Parson," John Chivington. Not only that, because of Sibley's plan, James Carleton was telegraphed to lead the California Column, 1,800 strong, east along the southern route to head off the Confederate invasion. By the time Carleton reached New Mexico Territory, the Rebels were gone, and his Californians and New Mexicans would fight Apache and Navajo instead.

But the nation would focus on a unique event involving American Indians before the frontier burst into hostilities. The Missouri Home Guard under Sterling Price, Texas regiments under former Ranger Benjamin McCulloch, and Arkansas volunteers prepared to march out of northern Arkansas and to win the state of Missouri once and for all for the Confederacy. Albert

Pike, not only an Indian commissioner but also a brigadier general in the Confederate Army, was convinced to lead three regiments and one battalion of the Indian troops from the Nations. They joined the Rebel army of Gen. Earl Van Dorn in west central Arkansas. Their column made an unforgettable spectacle as it approached Van Dorn's white soldiers. An open carriage led the march carrying old Cherokee John Ross in a broadcloth coat and a stovepipe hat; beside him was Pike dressed for propaganda purposes as a Plains Indian chieftain.

Van Dorn fell ill as he planned an envelopment of the Federal army of Gen. Samuel R. Curtis. Van Dorn issued orders from an ambulance in March 1862, at Pea Ridge in extreme northwestern Arkansas. In a blanket of snow, the gray troops fought Union troops through the day of March 7, 1862. The heaviest fighting on the first day of the battle on the part of the Northern troops fell on the shoulders of Missouri regiments of German-Americans under Brig. Gen. Franz Siegel.

The Indian soldiers of the Five Tribes participated mostly on the first day of fighting at Pea Ridge. The night before the battle Pike's Indian regiments took up a position on the Confederate right. That night as bivouac fires flamed high above the snow, the Rebel lines drew back, keeping the fires burning brilliantly to distract the Yankees into an envelopment. At midmorning on March 7 the Union troops advanced. Siegel's Germans, led by Prussian-trained Peter J. Osterhaus, were the first to encounter the Indian regiments. The Union troops, mostly volunteers from the vicinity of St. Louis, had advanced around the west side of a prominence called Round Top when they were brought abruptly face-to-face with an appalling aggregation of warriors in very loose ranks across an empty, snow-covered field. They were Pike's and Cooper's Indian commands, later dubbed by the Northern press as "The Aboriginal Corps of Tomahawkers and Scalpers."

The men of the Five Tribes were ill-armed, and clothed in civilian attire, some with high-crowned hats or forage caps decorated with feathers. One observer noted that the elder

Fighting at Pea Ridge.

statesmen among the Indian regiments looked like copper images of white men; the younger warriors with those headgears perched "on their High Heads of Hair . . . made rather a Comical Ludicrous appearance."

There was nothing comical about them at Pea Ridge that frosty morning. Their officers led Chickasaw and Choctaw, Seminole, Creek, and Cherokee in a wildly whooping assault. Osterhaus's Teutonic volunteers were barely able to unlimber a few cannon and fire a few shells before they were swamped. Texas cavalry led the way, and the Union Germans might have stood their ground against Texans, but close on their heels came John Drew's mounted and Stand Watie's dismounted Cherokee. The Federal horsemen fled headlong through the batteries and supporting infantrymen—soon the rout was complete. Thrilled with their easy victory and capture of the cannon, Drew's Cherokee celebrated. "With shouts of laughter they danced around the abandoned 'shooting wagons,' roaring delightedly as they held horse collars around their necks and pranced about with harness chains jingling."

The elation of the Cherokee encouraged Confederate Ben McCulloch to throw the Texas and Arkansas regiments into the fray. With Osterhaus's men in retreat, the regiments of Union Gen. Eugene A. Carr—whose name would be familiar to Plains Indians for the rest of his long military career—were hard pressed. Despite having the first of three wounds that he received dressed while he was in the saddle, Carr held the line stoutly, bolstered the retreating men of Osterhaus, and called for desperately needed reinforcements. General Curtis sent the help, but even that could not have covered the Federal lines had Carr not stubbornly held his ground.

General Pike realized that the fight was not over. He urged the Five Tribesmen to charge again. They paid him no heed, convinced the white soldiers had run away. Then more Union artillery opened a hot fire on their position. The First Cherokee and the Second Cherokee regiments took this shelling and found themselves on the defensive behind trees and rocks. The dreaded cannon fire demoralized Drew's men, who once more began looking for opportunities to go over to the Union. Stand Watie's men sniped at them, determined to prevent desertions.

As Pike feared, once reinforced Osterhaus's German infantry regained their courage and charged to recapture the guns. In the hard fighting of the wintry March afternoon Confederate Gen. Ben McCulloch was killed, and shortly thereafter so was his second in command, white Gen. James McIntosh. The Yankees, securing themselves in the lines they had abandoned in such a hurry near midday, claimed to find at least eight scalped corpses. The Northern press made much of the old familiar horror. Some confirmation came, according to one historian, when a woman stated that scalps from the battle had been sent by mail to relatives in the Cherokee Nation. An infantryman in the Fifth Illinois Volunteers found his brother scalped on the field and claimed nine Reb scalps of his own during the next day's fighting.

Night fell on both sides, facing each other with not much difference in the lines from earlier in the day. The battle was rejoined on March 8, but the Indians had only a small role. Drew's regiment left the lines and soon headed for home. The remaining Choctaw, Chickasaw, Seminole, and Creek wavered irresolutely, disorganized and without orders. Only Stand Watie's Second Cherokee remained in control, and even they failed again under artillery fire. In fairness to the regiments of the Five Tribes, white outfits this early in 1862 behaved no more valorously, yet the Indians have been portrayed as ignorant savages because of their performance in combat at Pea Ridge. At the end of the battle, however, the retreating Southern army found Stand Watie's Second Cherokee still ready to serve. This Indian regiment helped cover the Rebel retreat, and Watie himself was on his way to earning a brigadier's star.

On April 19, Henry Hastings Sibley's Confederate army in New Mexico, too, was in retreat. Glorieta Pass had been a tactical victory, but due to Chivington's raid a strategic loss for the

Confederates. Sibley's brigade was shattered by the end of the campaign. Of about 2,500 men who composed the invasion force hardly more than 1,800 effectives returned to Texas. But Federal forces had been set in motion that would soon impact the Indians in the Southwest because of the Rebel invasion.

The Navajo *ladrones* were emboldened by the withdrawal of the white soldiers during the previous summer and autumn. Though poorly supplied with firearms and marginal bowmen at best, the Navajo were no easy opponents. They had been in contact with European cultures for longer than many American Indians and like the Five Civilized Tribes had adopted those characteristics that appealed to them. With most of the Federal troops gone and what was left preoccupied with Rebels on their doorsteps, the Navajo extensively raided the flocks and herds of settlers with Hispanic heritage. They also expanded their raiding, attacking supply trains, commercial caravans, and even isolated military posts with impunity.

At the same time, the Apache raided down from the mountains or up from the border with Mexico. Miners banded together and held Indian hunts. When they could trap Apache, they killed them to the last man—and the last woman and the last child too. The Apache, naturally, killed all the white and Mexican men who had the misfortune to fall into their hands. The few white women on the frontier might be raped and enslaved, or women and children alike could be adopted into the Apache bands. The cruel methods of the whites led to especially unusual torture by the Apache. Extermination became the way of war between whites and Indians, with each trying to outdo the other in mutilation and horror. So although the New Mexico Volunteers were organized and the California Column had been called east to defend against Rebels, they wound up fighting Indians instead. Until these units could bring their weight to bear, however, the Union had to use whatever it could get.

One such unit was a battalion of the Second Kansas Volunteers. The Second's colonel, Robert B. Mitchell, was wounded at Wilson's Creek, then promoted to brigadier general in April 1862. His old regiment was part of the brigade of Kansas regiments he was to command which assembled at Fort Riley. Abruptly in May 1862, both Mitchell and his brigade— except the Second Kansas—were ordered to Tennessee. Waiting at Fort Riley was a large accumulation of wagons whose owners hoped to accompany Mitchell's Kansans across the plains to New Mexico. None of the civilian freighters were willing to go it alone. An escort for this train was detailed including Companies A, C, and D of the Second Kansas.

Crossing the Kansas plains, the battalion found the Southern Cheyenne and Arapaho on the warpath. Company C was left to strengthen the shrunken garrison at Fort Larned— roughly the halfway point along the trail to Santa Fe. The very day—June 22, 1862—the other two companies reached Fort Union, New Mexico Territory, Capt. Samuel J. Crawford led the one hundred men of Companies A and D in pursuit of a band of Navajo who had killed some Mexican shepherds and stolen their flocks. Crawford and his short battalion punished the raiders, retrieved the sheep, and returned to Fort Union on June 27. They left on July 5, and two days out of Fort Larned they got a "hurry-up" dispatch that the fort was surrounded by hostile Indians and liable to be attacked at any moment. Crawford wrote that about three thousand "of the savage barbarians," the Cheyenne and Arapaho, had been swarming around the fort demanding sugar, coffee, flour, and bacon. A show of force and a powwow finally lifted the bloodless siege. Crawford took all three companies to man a new post at the Great Bend of the Arkansas River known along the the trail as the "Bloody Crossing" during August. The little battalion finally crossed the rest of Kansas to rejoin the rest of the Second Kansas at Fort Scott on September 20, 1862, "having traveled over two thousand miles" in five months.

In June 1862, as summer dried up the water holes and turned the little grass in the desert crisp, Apache noticed soldiers coming from the west instead of the east. Cochise called his Chiricahua and Mangas Coloradas gathered the Mimbres to cope with the large number of white men. The combined Apache force numbered about seven hundred Apache, the largest group of warriors the Apache ever mustered. Cochise and Mangas had their men line the slopes of Apache Pass, not far from where the Bascom affair had occurred, to ambush the California Column led by "General Jimmy" Carleton. The lead element of the Californians entered the meandering pass on July 15, headed for Apache Springs, which were the sole water sources for more than a day's ride in any direction.

Capt. Thomas F. Roberts, First California Infantry, led the advance unit, followed at some distance by part of the supply train under command of Capt. John C. Cremony. Three companies of infantry, a detachment of cavalry, two mountain howitzers, and the civilian freighters entered the pass with all proper precaution. As Roberts's command approached the overland mail station to which Cochise's people had once provided wood, a hail of bullets and arrows poured down on the bluecoats from both sides of the gap.

Thrown back by musket balls and feathered missiles, the Californians reformed into skirmishing lines and fought their way through the gorge to the stagecoach station. The Apache took cover behind rocks and stunted trees on the overlooking slopes to prevent the thirsty white soldiers from reaching the vital water of the springs, still some six hundred yards away. It had taken Roberts and his men several hours to get that far— the water was tantalizingly close, losses were slight, but the Apache held the high ground behind natural breastworks.

Hundreds of miles to the east, on a peninsula leading from Jamestown to Richmond, Virginia, other Union artillery massed on an incline at Malvern Hill blasted a Confederate assault to smithereens. Likewise, here in the West, Captain Roberts unlimbered his mountain howitzers. In haste to follow those orders, the artillerymen allowed one of the pieces to overturn, and Apache fire from above sent its crew scampering for shelter. Sgt. Titus B. Mitchell of the cavalry contingent led a half-dozen of his men on foot to the howitzer and returned it to its carriage, whereupon its crew came out from hiding, and both of the guns opened fire with explosive shells, and equally explosive results. "We would have done well enough," one Apache told a white officer later, "if you had not fired wagons at us."

The projectiles burst among the Apache warriors entrenched among the rocks. Until then, neither side had suffered severe casualties, but then the Apache were cut down in greater numbers than they had ever known before. It was too much for them, unused to the white soldiers' style of warfare. The explosions that filled the air with deadly flying lead balls quickly caused even the bravest among them to break and run.

Roberts pushed on through the pass to the springs and pitched camp, with extra videttes out ready for action in case the Indians returned. He took stock of the situation—one account reported sixty-three dead Apache, mostly shell-fire casualties, to two dead and two wounded soldiers—and sent word of the fight back to Captain Cremony. Once more Sergeant Mitchell with four of his horse soldiers drew the assignment. The cavalrymen had barely emerged from the pass to warn the approaching supply train than Mangas Coloradas himself, leading about fifty warriors, raced after them. In the running fight one sergeant with Mitchell was wounded, and three of the cavalry mounts went down. Two riders were picked up and rode double to safety. The third took cover behind his dead horse, loaded his single-shot, breech-loading carbine, drew his revolver, and prepared to sell his life dearly. He held the circling warriors off for nearly an hour before he got a clear shot. A large Apache took a slug, and then the rest of his foes rode away. He walked back to camp carrying his saddle and bridle, not knowing till later than it was the Mimbres leader, Mangas Coloradas, he had shot. His warriors carried the chief south into Chihuahua and forced a Mexican doctor to remove the slug. Meanwhile, Captain Roberts faced renewed fighting in Apache Pass the next day. This time, the fight was short and minor. The two cannon opened fire, driving the Apache away again with bursting shells.

The spirit of the white soldiers became clearer with each encounter. If the Indians had been able to see the broad perspective all across the American West rather than focusing on isolated, individual warfare, they might have understood the inexorable attitude of the Americans. Perhaps those of the Five Tribes had begun to grasp the changes to come. Soon, however, the indigenous people of the prairies, plains, mountains, and desert discovered that the soldiers would come back, this time in ever-increasing numbers, approaching the task of Indian fighting with vigor, aggressiveness, and brutality. Far from Apache Pass, another group of Indians learned the lesson within a month, but not before they had experienced some elated success.

All of July and half of August had passed, yet the annuity payment to the Santee Sioux had still not arrived in Minnesota. The agent declined to issue the food and general goods until the money arrived. What few provisions the Indians could get were poor or spoiled, while their own corn crop among the "farmer Sioux" was ruined by cutworms. When the Santee pleaded for food at the agency store, its proprietor, Andrew Myrick, sneered: "So far as I'm concerned, if they are hungry let them eat grass or their own dung."

The Santee leader, Little Crow, remonstrated with the white authorities. Many of his people thought him a pawn of the whites, but they still wanted him to lead them. Four Santee youth hunting north of Redwood Agency, Minnesota, forced the hand of Little Crow on August 17, 1862. The young men entered a farmyard on that quiet Sunday and killed five white settlers. The act was apparently unplanned, only a juvenile dare to prove their courage. The Santee challenged the farmers to a shooting match, magnanimously letting the whites shoot first. When their rifles were emptied, the Santee turned on them savagely, killing the three white contestants and two women.

For the Santee the issue of standing behind the boys provoked a stormy meeting in which all the pent-up wrath of a decade spilled over. Little Crow, fresh from church that Sunday, found himself listening to the boasts of the four boys, the excited

Santee Sioux beg for annuities at their agency.

"Let them eat grass."

militants, and a boisterous crowd of young warriors who had never had a chance to prove themselves. At last he reluctantly pledged to lead his people in the war to relieve the long-suppressed group.

At dawn on August 18, 1862, the Santee launched a surprise attack on the Redwood Agency and the store there. The white men were killed, the women and children were taken into captivity, and the buildings were torched. In a savage outbreak, parties of Santee spread over a 250-mile swath of countryside, slaughtering and destroying all that lay in their path. The Minnesota farmers were utterly surprised by the shocking ferocity, murder, rapine, pillage, and burning by the Indians, some of whom like Little Crow were Christian converts. By evening on August 18, almost five hundred white farmers had been killed, and hundreds more fled desperately toward Fort Ridgely. For example, of a party of twenty-eight ambushed on Sacred Heart Creek, only one survived to the safety of the fort. Among the dead that first day was agency head Andrew Myrick. His corpse was discovered mutilated and with its mouth ironically filled with grass, the very food he had recommended for the Santee.

Nothing seemed to prevent the swath of destruction from overwhelming St. Paul, the Minnesota state capital, itself. But the Santee split. Little Crow, a cautious tactician, knew that the greatest threat to the uprising lay with the handful of soldiers and the swelling number of male refugees at Fort Ridgely. The rest of the hungry Sioux were lured to the prosperous town of New Ulm and the prospect of booty.

Fort Ridgely was not the stereotypical log-stockaded frontier fort. A quadrangle of frame buildings surrounding the parade ground with its flagpole in the center was the main post, but single-story cabins and wooded ravines provided plenty of cover if the fort was ever attacked. As refugees inundated the post, one of its officers, Capt. John Marsh, assumed it was an isolated rebellion and set out with less than fifty soldiers of the roughly hundred-man garrison to bring it swiftly under control. He led his small force straight into an ambush at a river ferry nearby. A heroic ferryman had rescued scores of people there till he succumbed to the hostile Indian fire. Now they blazed away at Marsh's command from tall grass and brush-lined river banks. The captain was not killed by Indians while leading his men across a ford; instead, Marsh suffered a cramp, fell into deep water, and drowned. Only about half of the men who went out with March returned, and five of them soon died of their wounds.

The captain's demise left brave but inexperienced nineteen-year-old Lt. Thomas Gere in command. The fort then had about fifty effectives, plus some armed civilians. Pvt. William Sturgis rode 125 miles in eighteen hours to Fort Snelling. He and other desperately dispatched riders brought reinforce-ments to raise the strength to 180. They brought word of another battle too. In desperate fighting, a large war party of Sioux had been repulsed at the town of New Ulm. Civilian defenders had beaten back assaults by angry Santee. The Sioux had suffered heavy casualties and had finally left the heavy fighting for easier pickings around the countryside. To increase the irony of the situation, a stagecoach arrived at Fort Ridgely with the cash annuities for the tribe, the absence of which had been the final straw before the uprising.

It came too late. Fort Ridgely's garrison prepared for the worst. But the aging post had at one time housed ordnance for the frontier. There remained a 6-pounder, a pair of 12-pounders, and several 24-pounder howitzers kept in pristine condition by Ordnance Sgt. John Jones. The old cannon had much senti-mental value to Jones and the volunteers he used as gun crews, but they had never seen better days than those to come.

Minnesota had rarely seen the pageantry it witnessed on August 20, 1862, as Little Crow marshaled his Santee for an overwhelming onslaught. Only the cloudy, overcast weather dis-pelled the showy spectacle just beyond the simple cover the Sioux used to shield their infiltrations from the fort's defend-ers. It was almost a shame that the white people could not see the glamorous preparations. Instead, after five days of slaughter and bloodshed the men stood grimly at their posts in the fort, with Sergeant Jones's men at their pieces scattered strategically around at advantageous points and with a couple of reserve cannon on the grassy parade ground. Women begged their men to shoot them rather than let them fall into the hands of the vengeful Sioux. As raindrops began to pepper the prairies around Fort Ridgely, enough that fire arrows failed to ignite the roofs of the wooden structures, Little Crow's Santee warriors crept through underbrush and between shanties and cabins, reaching the outer defenses undetected.

With classic war whoops the Santee brushed aside the pitiful attempts of the white defenders to stop them. They stormed forward, several hundred strong, intent on destroying the barracks on the quadrangle and all within them. The scene became one of carnage. The latest commander at Fort Ridgely, Lt. Timothy Sheehan who had brought reinforcements from Fort Snelling, rallied his meager troops in a huddle on the parade ground for a last stand.

And then Sergeant Jones opened fire with his cannon. With shell and canister a 12-pounder spoke volumes as it belched death into the flank of the Santee assault. It was the turn of the Sioux to be surprised. They fell back in disarray. As they rallied under cover of the captured buildings, Jones and his gun crews fired more shells into their midst. One shell set a barn full of attackers ablaze. Canister—nasty cans filled with lead balls like shotgun shells—raked the undergrowth that concealed more assailants. A lucky shot by one of the big 24-pounders dropped right into the Santee encampment—shrapnel plowed a furrow in Little Crow's own scalp. Panic spread among the Santee noncombatants too.

But Fort Ridgely was not a fight of disorganized terror—it was a battle of push and shove between two hard-pressed but well-controlled and well-commanded foes. The Santee regrouped and continued pressing the attack. Lieutenant Sheehan's men fell back under the renewed pressure. When their ammunition ran low, they broke open the artillery's canister shells, using the powder and lead balls in their muskets. The

Santee were lucky enough on that damp and dreary day to touch off one dry haystack, and before long some of the woodpiles and small frame outbuildings burned too, filling the fort with choking amber smoke. From this smoke screen, a large group of Santee emerged, then rushed Sergeant Jones's barricaded cannon. Despite heavy musketry, the soldiers depressed the barrel and gave them point-blank "what for," then elevated it to shell trees hiding snipers. Sergeant McGee and his crew hauled their 24-pounder over next to the engaged piece, and both guns were double charged with some of the remaining canister.

When Little Crow launched his Santee in the largest attack at Fort Ridgely, accompanied by a strong supporting column, both guns blazed away rapid fire. Dozens if not scores of Indians went down, killed, wounded, or just dodging for cover. The guns boomed away, spewing a steady stream of balls until the Sioux wave ebbed and faded. Then McGee loaded his big howitzer with a large shell. It left the cannon barrel with a thunderous roar and exploded among the withdrawing Indians with an even louder explosion, splitting the Santee forward elements from their support. One of the white officers wrote how "the ponderous reverberations of the big gun echoed up the valley as though twenty guns had opened, and the frightful explosion struck terror to the savages."

That violent blast saved Fort Ridgely. But it did not break the Santee resistance—it would take flesh and blood men to do that. While Little Crow tried to reorganize his braves, former Gov. Henry Hastings Sibley was commissioned a colonel of Minnesota state militia. He mobilized between 1,400 and 1,500 very young or middle-aged militia and some civilian vigilantes, poorly armed and with only modest training and discipline, as a relief expedition. More than a few of the men who joined were bent on revenge.

Sibley told his successor as governor, Alexander Ramsey—like Sibley another white Minnesotan who had made a fortune plundering by graft the Santee Sioux cash annuities—that "[m]y heart is steeled against [the Sioux], and if I have the means, and can catch them, I will sweep them with the besom [broom] of death." Sibley and his hastily assembled relief column drove through scenes of carnage and destruction to the rescue of still-threatened Fort Ridgely and the nearly obliterated town of New Ulm. Despite Sibley's bombast, the Santee were determined, unrecalcitrant, and well supplied with a mixture of captured guns and ammunition. They also held about 250 white women and children hostages. Some Sioux caught an unwary burial party of Sibley's men and inflicted nearly 50 percent casualties before the colonel came to its aid. The lust for revenge ran high on both sides.

Sioux leaders continued to quarrel; Little Crow remained a reluctant war chief; and the Santee fell back before Sibley's advance. On September 23, 1862, the final major battle with the Santee at Wood Lake twice came close to disaster. Little Crow's warriors ambushed the white army's van from both flanks. The part-time white soldiers were battered and fell back in disorder. Sibley threw five companies forward in a rush to cover the retreat. Forced to a defensive position on a hilltop, the whites fended off repeated assaults for more than two hours. One of the Sioux charges boiled out of a covered ravine. Once more artillery came to the rescue as a pair of cannon blazed away with canister. At last the Indians drew off and scattered, finally demoralized, as Sibley's command—especially the artillery battery—drove them from the Wood Lake battlefield. The action proved decisive, and the Santee realized that their power was broken.

After the Battle of Wood Lake, the Santee released their hostages on the chance that it would lessen their inevitable punishment. The likelihood was small—the death toll of the Minnesota uprising stood at least eight hundred whites and was estimated by some as high as two thousand. The number of Sioux dead was never effectively tabulated. Many of the Santee who survived became fugitives and scattered to other Sioux bands in Dakota or north into Canada. Those who did not escape were unrelentingly hunted down by Sibley, now promoted to militia general. As the fall deepened toward winter, more than a thousand were captured or surrendered as military patrols scoured the countryside, ferreting out all Indians.

The Navajo watched the successes of other Indians and the successes of whites throughout 1862. By the middle of that year, the Southern white men had been repulsed, and new white soldiers in blue, General Carleton and his Californians, had arrived from the west. Not only that, since the Confederates were gone the New Mexico volunteers were free to turn their attention to Indians. The White Eyes from the west built new forts. Fort Bowie was a castle-like adobe fortress erected in 1862 to control Apache Pass, scene of that battle when those Indians brought together more warriors than they ever fielded till then or since. Closer to the Navajo, Fort Wingate was built on the edge of their country. Word came that bluecoat soldiers were soundly defeating the Mescalero east of the Rio Grande River.

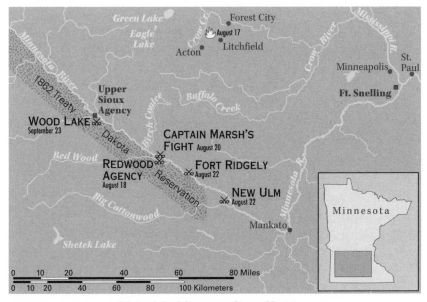

Map of the Minnesota Sioux Uprising.

Worried about their futures, eighteen *ricos* ventured to Carleton's headquarters at Santa Fe in December 1862. They wanted to talk to the soldier chief—Carleton had been placed in command of the entire Southwest. The general had no time for the expected ceremony and presents typical for such conferences—he dealt with them perfunctorily and bluntly. He ordered the Navajo to go back to their people and tell them he expected more than talk before he would consider them peaceful.

Actually, Carleton planned nothing less than complete conquest, absolute submission, and total control of all the Indian people within his reach. He took seriously his mission to keep open the southern routes of communication. From his home state east to Santa Fe, then onto the plains east of Fort Union and into the Texas Panhandle, Carleton planned to make the links safe from any threats. The Federal government had its hands full with the Southern rebellion; it did not need to worry about Indians on the frontier. The hammer that he would use was mountain man and now colonel of the First New Mexico Volunteers, Kit Carson.

Carson rounded up the troublesome bands of Mescalero, marching them from their mountain homeland to the most barren part of eastern New Mexico Territory in the Pecos River Valley—the infamous Bosque Redondo, "round grove of trees." Here, too, Carleton built Fort Sumner as a guard post over the virtual prisoners. With the Apache under his thumb, Carleton could plan the same fate for the Navajo.

At the end of 1862, much of the West seemed inflamed by Indian wars. The Chiricahua and Mimbres had seen a defeat, the Santee were on the run, the Five Tribes had suffered a setback at Pea Ridge. But the Plains Indians rampaged from Texas to Nebraska and into Dakota Territories, the Civilized Tribes produced an outstanding leader in Stand Watie, and the Navajo raided with impunity in spite of the peace efforts of the *ricos*. As the seasons blended together in the second year of the white men's war, the strikes by Indians in 1862 were swiftly followed by decisive action by bluecoat soldiers in 1863.

CHAPTER 3

"I Want Him Dead!": 1863

As the winter of 1862-63 deepened, Mangas Coloradas was again leading his Mimbres Apache against the Pinos Altos miners. He had recovered sufficiently from wounds he received at the Battle of Apache Pass to lead his men, though not without pain. But in January 1863, as both sides grew weary of fighting, Mangas allowed himself to be lured by a white flag of truce to parley with Col. Joseph R. West. This treacherous white officer in short order accomplished what hundreds of White-Eye soldiers had failed to do. West seized the giant Mangas Coloradas, accused the Apache leader of recently plundering a wagon train, and sent him from West's tent as a prisoner.

Within earshot of another soldier, West issued orders about Mangas to two soldiers: "Men, that old murderer has got away from every soldier command and left a trail of blood five hundred miles along the old stage line. I want him dead or alive tomorrow morning. Do you understand? I want him dead!"

That night, as Mangas Coloradas tried to sleep under guard by a campfire, the guards heated bayonets and touched them to the soles of the old chief's bare feet. Rising to his elbows in pain and angry protest, Mangas said he "was not a child to be played with." He was then cut down in a hail of musketry, pierced by four musket balls, killed, according to his captors, while attempting to escape. Then, as reported to one of the

Mangas Coloradas tortured with heated bayonets.

Pinos Altos miners who witnessed the events that night, the soldiers scalped and decapitated the old chieftain's corpse

White disdain and imprudence, even treachery such as that which killed Mangas Coloradas, touched off confrontations with many Southwestern tribes in 1863. Paiute were reported harassing travelers along the road near the California borders. Fort Mohave nearby was reported to be threatened by Mohave braves, but no attack developed. Even the small tribe of Chemehuevis along the Colorado River committed a few depredations, but nothing that a few patrols could not handle.

Apache also continued the struggle, goaded by the betrayal of Mangas Coloradas to even greater fury and cruelty. After the defeat at Apache Pass, Cochise never again attempted to mass his warriors, but he launched small war parties against travelers, miners, settlers, and isolated soldiers' patrols. These warriors wore their thick, glossy black hair bound about their temples with buckskin bands, white cloth, or brightly colored bandanas. They wore buckskin shirts or Mexican-style shirts and apron-like garments hanging from their waists to their knees. Their footwear was the knee-high *n'deh b'lech,* folded just below the knee, the thick-soled Apache moccasins. Their broad faces might be streaked with white clay or painted with natural pigments.

American troops who went after these wily warriors returned to their posts only to learn that the Apache they had thought they were chasing had doubled back and struck half a dozen places behind them or in another direction. They seemed to know the whereabouts and movements of almost all the soldiers and civilians in their hunting grounds. It became a war beyond any statistical accounting. A raid inspired by Cochise on a remote ranch or a small, lonely wagon train might claim a couple or a half-dozen lives; an attack on an Apache encampment could produce similar results. The Apache did not keep score, or at least were not consulted about the toll they took. Rumor and exaggerated reports by ambitious—or embarrassed—officers would count Apache casualties in the dozens and even scores.

In this kind of war, Gen. Jimmy Carleton had all he could handle. It was Colonel West and other Carleton subordinates who saw to it that Mangas Coloradas would lead no more attacks. Fiery Irishman Patrick Edward Connor, another Californian, had also led volunteers from his state east across the Great Basin to garrison the central overland route—the California branch of the Oregon Trail, Pony Express, and the transcontinental telegraph—and so wage war on the Indians who he believed threatened the tenuous link between California and the East.

From his headquarters at Camp Douglas overlooking Salt Lake City, the feisty Connor carried on a war of words with the Mormon Church and government leaders. Six years earlier President James Buchanan had sent Federal troops to Utah Territory when the appointment of a non-Mormon governor to replace Brigham Young caused trouble. Young had led the early Mormon settlement in the area and served as governor of Utah Territory from its organization in 1850 until 1857. Mormon militia burned U.S. Army wagon trains and harassed the lines of communication along the California Road that branched off of the Oregon Trail past Salt Lake City through Utah Territory, but before the two sides met in actual combat the "Mormon War" was settled by compromise. The only fighting in the war was the Mountain Meadows Massacre when Mormon militiamen and some Shoshone or Ute allies slaughtered about 120 members of an emigrant train outbound en route to California. After that event, the Mormons—used to persecution by other Americans—tried to stay neutral in the escalating slavery controversy. To many Northerners and abolitionists, however, neutrality was tantamount to treason. Connor was no exception and waged a bloodless but nonetheless vigorous feud with Brigham Young and other Mormon leaders.

Connor's California cavalry had little opportunity for action early in the war. They chased a few raiding Ute and patrolled Utah Territory and western Colorado Territory. But about the time Mangas Coloradas was killed in Arizona Territory, Connor demonstrated that he could go about Indian fighting with the same gusto, persistence, and lack of compassion as the best (or the worst) of them.

The Shoshone originally lived in the Great Basin between the Rocky Mountains and the Sierra Nevada, surviving on the meager resources of the virtual desert lands. About a century and a half before the Civil War, some Shoshone acquired horses and moved northeast to the plains and vast herds of buffalo in Wyoming. In winter, some moved south into the shelter of the northern Utah mountains. Although sometimes known as Snake Indians, the Shoshone were usually friendly to the whites.

Some of these people from the lodges of a Shoshone leader named Bear Hunter had been begging coffee, sugar, and tobacco from immigrants on the trail to California and miners headed toward the silver strikes in Nevada. They were hardpressed to sustain themselves in the brutal winter months. When settlers and travelers complained, Connor initiated a punitive expedition against Bear Hunter's village at Bear River, in north central Utah Territory. One frigid morning in January 1863, Connor and several companies of his Californians dashed across the frozen ground and attacked Bear Hunter's lodges. In a short, bloody, one-sided fight, Connor proved himself equal to Carleton's merciless brand of Indian fighting. His men smashed the Shoshone village, burned tepees, dispersed the pony herd, and left the shocked chief and more than two hundred of his people dead on the snow-covered ground. The Californians rode back to Camp Douglas in triumph, brandishing Shoshone scalps. The route through Wyoming and Utah Territory was safe from those Indians.

The Apache and Navajo wars in the Southwest, the hostilities on the High Plains, the participation of the Civilized Tribes in the Rebel army, and the Minnesota Sioux uprising caused the Federal commanders to consider ingenious, almost desperate, measures to beef up supplies of troops for the frontier. Perhaps as early as autumn 1862, a scheme had been proposed to use Confederate parolees against the Indians. In February

1863, the commander of the Union prisoner of war Camp Butler, Illinois, reported the presence of a great number of Irish, German, and Polish captives. Some of them had gone to the South to find work before the outbreak of the war. According to the Camp Butler commandant, "They are willing to take the oath of allegiance and fight for the Union, and but for the misfortune of locality would ere this be found in the ranks of loyal regiments." It would be more than a year before there would be results from such proposals.

As early as July 1862, U.S. Secretary of War Edwin M. Stanton authorized U.S. Marshal Robert Murray to interview prisoners of war in New York "for the purpose of ascertaining whether any and how many are willing to enter into the military services of the United States." Later that summer the commissary general of prisoners, William Hoffman, told the Federal adjutant, Lorenzo Thomas, that some Southern prisoners wished "to remain at the North and enter our service." Hoffman obviously recognized a way to alleviate the logistical responsibility of caring for large numbers of Confederate prisoners of war, a long-term commitment that the Union had not planned for when the war broke out. And on August 5, 1862, Indiana Gov. Oliver P. Morton wrote to Gen. Henry Halleck, commander of Federal forces, that a few Rebels of the many being held at Camp Morton "desire to volunteer into our Army instead of being exchanged."

Secretary Stanton could not make up his mind on the issue of enlisting prisoners until the Sioux uprising in Minnesota. From that state Governor Ramsey fired a bombardment of requests for troops to deal with Little Crow and his warriors, but the War Department had no troops to spare for fighting Indians. One Confederate army was invading Kentucky and even threatening Federal forces along the Ohio River in an attempt to relieve the pressure of the Union armies trying to close the Mississippi River; another was driving Gen. John Pope and the Yankees in the Army of the Potomac back nearly into the Washington, D.C., defenses. After Pope was relieved of his command following the debacle at Second Manassas, Stanton sent him to Minnesota to redeem himself.

Pope was a politically connected general, and the politicians who supported him likely convinced President Lincoln to appoint him commander of the Army of the Potomac. Pope was also a boastful man, and he probably convinced his supporters that he was a more qualified commander than he really was. He exaggerated his dispatches from the field with the headlines: "Headquarters in the Saddle." His Confederate opponent, Gen. Robert E. Lee with the Rebel Army of Northern Virginia, called Pope a miscreant after the braggart Yankee promised Lincoln he would "bag the whole lot" of Lee's army on the site of the war's first major battle in Virginia. He failed; Second Manassas was a crushing defeat for the Army of the Potomac, and Washington, D.C., was threatened by the Southern army. For this loss, Pope was ordered to Minnesota, about as far from the war's main theater of engagement as possible. By the time Pope arrived in the state that had been terrorized by the Santee Sioux uprising, the Indians had been defeated in open battle.

Pope had an opportunity to redeem himself by bringing order after the Sioux uprising. While badly factionalized and retreating westward onto the plains, there was still plenty of fight left in the Santee. Little Crow struggled to protect the lives of some one hundred captives still held by his warriors, some of whom were mixed-blood relatives of the Sioux. Secretary of War Stanton considered a suggestion from Minnesota's Governor Ramsey to help Pope control the remaining insurgents. "The 3rd Regiment of Minnesota Volunteers is on parole at Benton Barracks, St. Louis. We need a well-drilled force of which we are now utterly destitute to resist the overwhelming force of Indians now attacking our frontier settlements. Cannot you order the 3rd Regiment to report at once to me, with arms and ammunition, of which we are in great need? This service would not be in violation of their parole. The exigency is pressing."

The Secretary tended to agree with Governor Ramsey. The parole system arranged between the Union and the Confederacy provided that when either side secured an excess of prisoners of war they could be paroled and sent home, guaranteeing that they would no longer engage in hostilities against their captors. Ramsey's point was that almost an entire regiment of Minnesotans had been paroled—they would not violate the promise made if instead of fighting Rebels they fought Little Crow's Sioux warriors. By October 1863, Stanton had conferred with General Halleck when Confederates learned of the plan to use parolees against Indians. When the Southerners managed to bring it to the attention of President Lincoln, along with the addition of a no-Indian fighting clause to their parole documents, Halleck and Stanton replied by telegraph "that the parole under the cartel does not prohibit doing service against the Indians." The next day the Confederate government sent a message protesting the Yankee proposal to use parolees on the frontiers, quoting the parole agreement: "The surplus prisoners not exchanged shall not be permitted to take up arms again, nor to serve as military police or constabulary force in any fort, garrison or field work held by either of the respective parties, nor as guards of prisoners, depots or stores, nor to discharge any duty usually performed by soldiers, until exchanged under the provisions of this cartel." The Confederates feared on one hand that using parolees in these capacities would free other Yankee manpower to be loosed on them—and they were already feeling the pressure of weight of numbers against them—while on the other hand having parolees serving again only on the frontier could bring the former prisoners into direct conflict with some Confederate troops who happened to be Indians from the Five Civilized Tribes. Yet in Minnesota at that time, Pope had collected a mixed force of militia, volunteers, and a handful of regulars to put down the uprising.

By then the Sioux were leaderless. Little Crow had fled with a few followers north across the border into Canada. There he found little sympathy and no aid. After a brief, fruitless sojourn in America's northern neighbor, he returned with his son to their former home in Minnesota. On July 3, 1863, a frontier farmer near Hutchinson, Minnesota, caught the two Santee picking berries. Without so much as knowing who they were, he threw down and fired on them. Little Crow was mortally wounded. The reluctant Santee leader died of his wound later that afternoon. His son draped his remains in a blanket, then left without burying it. The Minnesota legislature voted the farmer a five-hundred-dollar reward for killing the chieftain.

With the Santee leaderless, and realizing that their power was broken, Pope supervised the mop-up operations that had been started by Henry Sibley. As the white soldiers hunted down small bands of individuals, many Sioux escaped across the western border of Minnesota into Dakota Territory. The roundup eventually netted about two thousand Santee. They were tried by a huge mass court-martial that sentenced 306 of them to death by hanging. Only a last-minute plea directly to Abraham Lincoln saved the majority of those convicted when the president reduced their penalties. Those who had simply fought in a battle were treated as prisoners of war. Nevertheless, thirty-eight who had also been convicted of murder, rape, or both were hanged in the "largest legal group execution in American history."

The fate of the Santee Sioux failed to dampen the warlike spirit of the Plains Sioux—indeed, if anything it roused their hostile ardor. They had seen their cousins the Santee herded onto a reservation and wanted no part of that. Untrammeled, they also saw the opportunity the war between the whites gave them. Pope would soon have to deal with other formidable Indian enemies, and he would command some of his former white enemies in the campaign.

The year 1863 was a turning point in the war for the Union armies. After an ignoble start with defeats at Fredericksburg and Chancellorsville in Virginia, and with Gen. Ulysses S. Grant's Yankee army stymied along the Mississippi River, the

Execution of thirty-eight Santee Sioux.

victories at Gettysburg and Vicksburg and at Helena, Arkansas, in the Trans-Mississippi West turned the tide. Meanwhile, Indians took care of another, smaller group of Rebels on the prairies of Kansas.

Charley Harrison, noted shootist from Arkansas who had risen to the role of leader among the Southern sympathizers, who were called "bummers," in Denver, Colorado Territory, decided his followers needed more organization and needed to be legitimized. Almost one-third of the gold rush boomtown's population was from the South. In the spring of 1863, Harrison and about twenty of his most ardent supporters rode south to the Santa Fe Trail at the Big Timbers, a large stand of cottonwoods along the Arkansas River. Then the riders headed east on the trail to the nearest organized Confederate army, located then in Harrison's home state of Arkansas.

Harrison and his men sought commissions from some Rebel higher command to legitimize themselves and to make them part of the Southern military forces. Then they could organize their followers into a guerrilla force similar to that of William Clarke Quantrill. The Southerners in Colorado Territory could wreak havoc in the gold fields, or arouse the Plains Indians to attack isolated Yankee posts, or draw Federal troops from the Eastern fronts, or earn personal gain and position in Colorado Territory if the South were to win the war.

The bummers were not much different from many of the other gold rush, boomtown Coloradans in and around Denver with regard to their respect for Indians—of which they had very little. They showed the Southern Cheyenne and Arapaho and, in southeast Kansas, the Osage how white men dealt with their kind on their way east. In mid-May, Harrison secured commissions for his men, probably from Gen. Sterling "Old Pap" Price, and headed back to Denver. From Arkansas the band of new Confederate officers crossed southwest Missouri and southeastern Kansas, cautiously avoiding Yankee patrols.

Once past the settled parts of southeastern Kansas, they felt safe to ride openly and in a direct line for the Santa Fe Trail.

Harrison's Rebels had trespassed on the Osage Reserve on their way east, and they crossed it again on their way home. Some of the Osage argued with members of the Southern party on the way east. In the heated exchange that followed, someone shot an Osage. The Osage, under their leader, Hard Rope, were waiting for the whites on the return trip.

The Osage who inhabited southeastern Kansas were considerably different from the Southern Cheyenne, the Arapaho, and the Ute with whom Harrison's small band were familiar. The tall, handsome warriors who roached their hair had been pushed west by white settlement for generations, from their homeland along the Mississippi River in Missouri and Arkansas to a reservation on the prairies of Kansas. The Osage warriors eagerly awaited the return of the brash, rude, violent Colorado guerrillas who had so deeply offended the Indians. They sought a chance to even the score. The chance came as Harrison's men approached the banks of the Verdigris River in southeastern Kansas.

About one hundred fifty Osage with Hard Rope caught up to the Coloradans and attacked with a few rifles, old muskets, and bows and arrows, killing one. The attackers were driven back, but some of the Osage were armed with long-range trade rifles while the Confederates carried mainly sidearms. Harrison and his men fled for the protection of the steep Verdigris River and Drum Creek banks. It became a running battle.

Even the cover of the stream banks was inadequate defense against the overwhelming numbers of the still-wild Osage. Two of them who had acquaintances in the Second Kansas Indian Home Guard regiment turned up at the Union post in Humboldt, Kansas, and casually reported the massacre of the white Rebels. All but two of Harrison's band were found later by members of the Ninth Kansas Cavalry regiment; the remains had been stripped, scalped, and mutilated. Charley Harrison himself had been balding, so his luxurious beard was scalped from his chin instead of having his topknot lifted. Two of the Rebels, one a relative of explorer Meriwether Lewis, believed their luck had run out when they had fallen behind in the vital ride for cover—instead, the Osage passed them by, making that one of the luckiest days of their lives.

The two survivors concealed themselves in the timber along the Drum Creek and Verdigris River banks until evening. Then, on a dark night with only stars to light their way, they walked across the prairie through the Osage Reserve, past the Yankee outposts along the state line between Kansas and Missouri. They made their way finally to the Confederate lines in Arkansas where they shared their side of the story.

Some writers claim that Harrison wanted the commission in the Confederate Army to further his plans to arouse the Plains tribes into hostility against the Federal troops on the plains. However, it is just as likely that Federals concocted that excuse to lay blame at the Rebel doorstep while avoiding the responsibility for bringing on the Indian war that smoldered briefly, then ignited on the plains the next spring. In fact, before the Civil War and early in the conflict between whites, the frontier settlers often got along well with the Plains Indians.

On the plains, Christiana Phillips was the only white woman in Salina, the westernmost town in Kansas, halfway across the state. While her menfolk were away at the war or trading, Mrs. Phillips tended the family's trading post, gathering pelts, buffalo robes, and furs. The Southern Cheyenne called her "White Sister" and respected her, because she never sold them alcohol, never did business on Sunday, and although patient with them was always firm and honest.

She treated Indians the same as whites, once chasing off drunken white volunteer soldiers at gunpoint for chasing two Kansa into her house for refuge. She brought tears of laughter to Indian women with some of her white female antics, yet on the other hand treated a sick Indian woman with castor oil only to find the young squaw delivered twins shortly after her medication.

Knowing the Plains Indians as they did, some frontier people

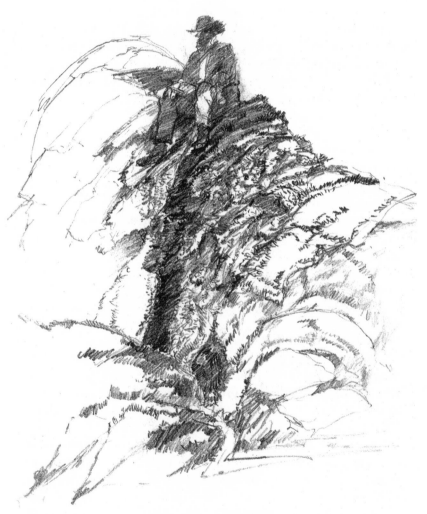

Buffalo hides on the plains.

were critical of the policies pursued by those representing the Federal government. Since any documents Charley Harrison's party might have carried conveniently disappeared, it was easy to blame those dead victims who had happened to be on the losing side of the war of inflaming the frontier. The war in the East was approaching a turning point in the summer of 1863, but the war on the High Plains was just beginning.

Rebel guerrillas were the greatest threat to Kansas and Missouri in 1863, including a raid in May 1863, as far west as Diamond Springs, the first campground west of Council Grove on the Santa Fe Trail. In light of that raid and Harrison's demise in the Drum Creek massacre, along with growing unrest among the Southern Cheyenne and Arapaho, there was cause for concern about keeping open the lines of communication along the Santa Fe Trail.

The Yankee commander in the district most affected by the Confederate guerrillas was a Kansan, Gen. James G. Blunt. Blunt's solution to the bushwhacker problem was to adopt a policy of public executions to punish guerrillas while at the same time placating furious Unionists. Blunt's policy escalated the guerrilla warfare, causing first the splitting of Blunt's district into two smaller ones, and then the Kansas general's removal to the plains where he commanded only a few hundred men scattered at small posts in company-sized or smaller units. Blunt considered his removal to the plains as banishment for his harsh policy, but there was a real worry about the threat to the Santa Fe Trail. The Kansas general was expected to maintain order on the trail with only some three hundred Iowa and Wisconsin volunteers and a few local militiamen from his headquarters at Fort Riley, Kansas. While there was much friction between red men and white, there were no major battles yet.

That was not the case in Blunt's old command headquarters at Fort Scott, Kansas. There, Col. William Phillips, another Kansan, commanded the Kansas Indian Brigade, which consisted of the First, Second, and Third Kansas Indian Home

Guard regiments. These Indian regiments—partly Union-sympathizing refugees from Indian Territory, partly recruits from reservations in Kansas—joined part of the Sixth Kansas Volunteer Cavalry, the Second Colorado Volunteers under Col. James Ford, the First and Second Kansas Colored Volunteer Infantry, and some companies of Wisconsin and Iowa regiments to fend off Confederate Texans, Confederate Indians, and Confederate guerrillas in Indian Territory and southern Kansas.

About the time the Osage got word that Charley Harrison's party was traversing their reservation again on their way home to Denver, five regiments of Rebel Indians and Texans crossed the Arkansas River and besieged Phillips in Fort Gibson, Indian Territory. A relief column of three hundred army wagons was organized at Fort Scott and set out for Fort Gibson. About halfway from Fort Scott to Fort Gibson lay a small Union outpost at the hamlet of Baxter Springs where the column was joined by the First Kansas Colored Infantry and an escort of parts of each of the three Union Kansas Indian regiments and the Sixth Kansas Cavalry under Maj. John Forman of the Third Indian Home Guard. Rebel Indian Col. Stand Watie's scouts soon detected the large force moving south, and the wily Cherokee colonel placed a troop at the ford of the military road across Cabin Creek.

On July 2, 1863, the same day armies east of these faced off against one another at Vicksburg and at Gettysburg, some Union Cherokee foiled Watie's surprise attack. Rain and high water slowed the Federal column's progress, allowing the Union leaders time to plan to thwart Stand Watie's Southern Indian troops. Leaving a force of white cavalry to defend the stockaded wagons, arranged in several concentric circles, the rest of the mixed lot of regiments slogged through the mud to secure the ford.

Cannoneers of the Second Kansas Light Artillery battery fired a half-hour barrage before Major Forman led mounted Federal Indians in an attack through the brimming Cabin Creek and against the entrenched Confederate Indian rifles.

Union riflemen provided a withering cover fire as the Ninth Kansas Cavalry charged across the ford as their Indian companions had done. They gained a foothold on the Rebel-held creek banks.

Next, Col. John Williams led the First Kansas Colored Volunteers in an infantry assault, first wading the chest-deep Cabin Creek holding their rifles high over their heads, then throwing their soaked bodies on the Rebel Indians. Despite a hail of bullets from the Rebel Indians, Watie's lines finally collapsed, and his Cherokee fled. Some drowned swimming the flooding Grand River south of the battlefield. Total Confederate Indian losses were unknown, but Federal casualties amounted to three dead and thirty wounded. The train and its escorts arrived safely at Fort Gibson two days after Union Indians engaged Confederate Indians at the Battle of Cabin Creek.

While this was occurring in the eastern portion of the Trans-Mississippi, things were heating up on the Western plains and in New Mexico. By the spring of 1863, most of the Mescalero Apache had surrendered to Gen. James Carleton's troops in the field—specifically, the First New Mexico Volunteers led by legendary Kit Carson, whose attention was then directed at recalcitrant Navajo.

Not all Navajo were hostile or raiders. Navajo peace leaders Barboncito and Delgadito met with General Carleton. He talked as bluntly as he had the previous December—all Navajo who wanted peace had to go live at Bosque Redondo, the desolate Pecos River valley reservation. Unable to bear the thought of moving their people to the veritable desert prison, the peace chiefs declined, but in June, Carleton repeated his ultimatum when he sent directions to the commander at Fort Wingate: "Tell them they can have until the twentieth day of July of this year to come in—they and all those who belong to what they call the peace party; *that after that day every Navajo that is seen will be considered as hostile and treated accordingly*; that after that day the door now open will be closed."

As winter approached, Carson mustered his First New Mexico Cavalry for another campaign against the Navajo who did not move to the Bosque Redondo and the others who continued to resist and raid. Some of the tribesmen fled with their families to a natural redoubt, a great gorge called Canyon de Chelly. It was dubbed the "Gibraltar of Navajodom," which, one officer warned, "no white command should enter."

Carson was undaunted. Since the Mexican War, he had been an Indian agent. New Mexico was his home, and he knew the territory well. He also knew how to fight Indians. Unorthodox and unused to the strictness and detail of military life, he detailed an experienced volunteer and First New Mexico trooper to take care of paperwork. The rest of the regiment were men of a different order. These were self-reliant frontiersmen and enlisted men who often had Mexican heritage.

Now, as the year 1863 drew toward a close, the campaign planned by Carleton and carried out by Carson and his men was designated to end the last resistance of the Navajo, to round them up and march them to the Bosque Redondo. Since 1861, Carleton and Carson had harried and hunted down the *ladrones* as well as the *ricos*. The Navajo were poorly supplied with guns, and though they were outcast even among other tribes like the Apache, Ute, and Pueblo, still the Navajo were no easy conquest. Yet in two years, numbers, perseverance, and depletion of resources gradually prevailed over them. Hogans, the Navajo earthen lodges, were destroyed, women and children taken prisoner, flocks captured. Trapped warriors surrendered or were wiped out. Yet Canyon de Chelly remained impregnable. Until the Navajo confidence in it as a defensive refuge was destroyed, they would never be subjugated.

Carson and his soldiers thrust deep into Navajo country north as far as Canyon de Chelly, west to the land of the Hopi, and south to the Little Colorado River. The white and Mexican soldiers carried out a scorched-earth policy, which would be emulated in the East the next year with Gen. William Tecumseh Sherman's march to the sea through Georgia.

Carson's troops were joined by those Indians who had shunned the Navajo before, Ute, Pueblo, Zuni, the usually temperate Hopi, even some Apache, and by white civilian vigilante groups who joined as much for profit as for their own defense.

Farther east, future foes of Carson were also active. On the plains of west Texas, along the Santa Fe Trail in New Mexico Territory and Kansas, in southeastern Colorado Territory, the tribes of the Southern Plains grew increasingly restless and hostile. The Southern Cheyenne, the Arapaho, the Kiowa and Comanche, enraged by the continuing intrusions and devastation, not to mention the high-and-mighty attitude of white men, fell on the few settlers and more often on travelers. Convinced that the withdrawal of regular troops from the plains at the outset of the war marked some success, the Kiowa had picked up the tempo and ferocity of their raids into Texas. The Comanche had considered Texans hereditary enemies and even differentiated between Americans and Mexicans on one hand and the despised Texans on the other. In western Kansas and along the Front Range of the Rocky Mountains, Cheyenne and Arapaho were antagonized by the brash, boorish, superior, and cavalier attitudes of Colorado miners and bullwhackers on the Santa Fe Trail.

The turning point of the war between the whites occurred in 1863 at Gettysburg and Vicksburg, east of the Mississippi River, and at Helena, Arkansas, and Cabin Creek in the Trans-Mississippi West. But there was still plenty of fight left in the Confederacy—the year 1863 also saw the Rebel victories at Chancellorsville in Virginia and Chickamauga in Georgia, and on the Kansas-Missouri border the devastating raid led by guerrilla William Clarke Quantrill on Lawrence. But on the Indian frontier the war was just beginning to flare into flames that would blaze here and there across the West for the next two decades. While many gazes were fixed on events in the East, the next year would bring new challenges to both red men and white men in the West.

Canyon de Chelly.

CHAPTER 4

"Soldiers Have Again Covered Themselves with Glory": 1864

In the deepening winter of January 1864, Carson and his men intensified the campaign against Canyon de Chelly and the Navajo therein. The war among white men continued to be prosecuted on many fronts, and white men everywhere in the country except the frontier were embroiled in it. National elections due for November of that year dominated many conversations. On the Indian frontier, speculation was rife about the renewal of hostilities with numerous tribes in many locations.

But the Indians in their winter camps were also troubled by the warfare on their Western frontier that had nothing to do with the Confederacy. This still seemed their best chance to throw the white intruders back where they came from. The optimism caused by the dwindling numbers of white soldiers in the West was tempered by the tenacity and cavalier attitudes of those remaining. They posed a serious threat to the families, lives, livelihoods, and homes of the Indians, whether those homes were tepees, earth lodges, pueblos, hogans, or wickiups.

The attack by William Clarke Quantrill's Rebel guerrillas on Lawrence, Kansas, gave people in towns west of the Missouri River pause. Throughout the West, public meetings were held to discuss various plans for defense from bushwhackers. On the frontier in most cases all that was done was to alert militia for possible service against the Indians. Even when the threat was imminent, discussion was often as far as most defense plans went during 1864. The frontier was reorganized on the first day of that year. On January 1, largely at the urging of Kansas Sen. James H. Lane, it was announced that President Abraham Lincoln had created a separate military department, the Department of Kansas, under the command of Gen. Samuel R. Curtis. The new department included the state of Kansas, Nebraska and Colorado Territories, and part of New Mexico Territory.

The rest of New Mexico Territory fell under Gen. Carleton's bailiwick. In that jurisdiction there had been much more activity. Kit Carson's First New Mexico and his Indian and civilian allies had thrust deep into Navajo country, according to one authority killing seventy-right people, wounding forty more, and rounding up about five thousand head of sheep, goats, and mules. Now Carson's forces were poised at the brink of the last bastion of that proud nation, Canyon de Chelly.

Colonel Carson's command consisted of 650 infantry and cavalry of Carleton's 1stFirst California and his own First New Mexico, two mountain howitzers that could be dismantled and carried on pack mules, Ute and Mescalero Apache scouts, and a supply train drawn by sturdy but slow oxen. With that force he proposed to subdue an estimated 10,000 Navajo in their strongest citadel.

The Navajo were not the only obstacles the white column confronted. Heavy snow slowed the oxen to a snail's pace of a mere five miles per day; twenty-five of the beasts died of exhaustion in as many miles. Cavalry horses faltered as grain gave out, forage disappeared with no grazing available, and some collapsed and had to be destroyed. Occasional brushes with the Navajo who made only brief defensive stands before retreating further impeded the column's progress toward the canyon.

At last Carson's troops closed on Canyon de Chelly itself. Detachments of bluecoat soldiers broke off to seal its entrance and any other means of entry—or more important, egress—as well as manning the rim with a thin line of white men. Colonel

Carson's subordinates were thorough planners, and they left little to chance, and even less chance for any Navajo to escape. At one end, a party of soldiers entered the canyon along an incredibly steep trail.

"The descent was truly terrific," one of them wrote. "We were four hours getting down the 800-foot depth. Mules fell distances from twenty to forty feet. Two were killed and several only saved their loads which prevented them from striking the rocks in their fall. Looking up it seemed as if there was no escape. The stream was running in the canyon, though often, the Indians say its bed is dry. Tall pines looked like bushes when contrasted with the sides of this *descensus averni*. Men and animals on the top, as seen from below, were like mites in the sky."

While these troops were clambering down the impossible trail, others with Colonel Carson forced the western entrance to the canyon. As the enraged Navajo fired arrows and bullets from old trade muskets from hiding places on the walls of the sheer red sandstone walls, the bluecoat soldiers thrust through the canyon. The Navajo fell back before them when faced with superior weapons, discipline, and strategy. A party of the Navajo who attempted to escape through a side canyon was met by fifty white men led by Sgt. Andreas Herrera, a New Mexican noncom often mentioned in dispatches. The blue columns on the canyon rims paralleling the Navajo retreat assured they could not scale the cliffs, while Carson's troops navigated the sandy floor of the canyon. The last hope for the Navajo was through the eastern natural gateway.

But Carson had cautiously provided for that eventuality. A force commanded by a redoubtable Indian fighter, Capt. Alfred Pfeiffer, who had given the Apache fits in 1862 and 1863, closed in on the eastern entrance. The trap had closed on the hapless Navajo.

Captain Pfeiffer, his soldiers, and a pack train moved into the gateway from the east in a difficult forced march in severe cold. Some hard-working volunteers led the advance guard, opening a narrow, hard-won path through the snowdrifts. The captain's force then wriggled into the canyon and thrust forward. The going was so difficult that pack train mules broke through the thick ice covering the stream that wended its way through Canyon de Chelly—the belly of one of them was slashed open by the sharp, jagged ice. Captain Pfeiffer pressed on regardless. The bastion made from a defile rang with shots of both soldier and Indian firearms; whistling arrows sliced through the frigid January air.

While Pfeiffer worked his way into the canyon from the east, and soldiers lined the rim to prevent escape of any Navajo, Kit Carson and the main force pushed ever deeper into Canyon de Chelly. From shallow caverns in the canyon walls and ledges lining the route the white men took, Navajo rained arrows and bullets on their enemy. War whoops and curses in pidgin Spanish accompanied every loose object at hand hurled on the heads of the soldiers. At one point in the struggle Captain Pfeiffer observed a Navajo woman heaving rocks and logs as diligently as the warriors. The captain's wife had been killed by Indians, and now he aimed his rifle and fired without compunction. The woman fell along with several warriors dropped by accurate fire. Resistance in front of the captain's troops died away.

Meanwhile, Colonel Carson's column fought its way through the canyon from the other direction. Shouting, whooping Navajo bawled brazen insults in broken Spanish and fired a few old muskets and rained hundreds of arrows from the red sandstone cliffs. Carson's men negotiated the treacherous, sandy canyon floor. They eventually rounded up a large flock of sheep and goats, and they destroyed orchards and food reserves wherever they found these sustaining products. A group of about sixty Navajo surrendered at one point to Carson's bluecoats, admitting, as Carson reported to General Carleton, that "owing to the operations of my command they are in a complete state of starvation and that many of their women and children have already died from this cause."

Pfeiffer's command met Carson's column midway in the

canyon. Remarkably, despite the brutal cold, the hardships of travel, and the attacks by Navajo, neither group had suffered any casualties. Carson successfully executed his plan for conquering Canyon de Chelly in spite of its legendary invincibility. The fighting spirit of most of the Navajo was finally broken. Captures and mass surrenders brought about due to starvation ushered an inundation of demoralized Indians into the hands of Carson's men. By the middle of March 1864, between 6,000 and 8,000 were corralled and camped under guard around Fort Canby and Fort Wingate in New Mexico Territory, awaiting removal to the Bosque Redondo reservation on the Pecos River. The bluecoat soldiers organized the "Long Walk," the understatement Navajo called their journey into exile on the arid Pecos bottomland. In groups of one hundred, white men guarding them, the columns of twos and threes—men, women, children—with horses, flocks of sheep, and mules or burros moved sadly eastward. It was a painful, in some cases a fatal way.

General Carleton's report to the Indian Department included observations of an experienced officer touched with pity:

> The exodus of this whole people from the land of their fathers is not only an interesting but a touching sight. They have fought us gallantly for many years; they have defended their mountains and stupendous canyons with a heroism which any people might be proud to emulate; but when it was their destiny, as it has been that of their brethren, tribe after tribe, to give way to the insatiable progress of our race, they threw down their arms. As brave men and fully entitled to our admiration and respect, they have come to us with confidence in our magnanimity; with the belief that we are too powerful and too just a people to repay that confidence with meanness or neglect. They hope that in return for having sacrificed to us their beautiful country, their homes, the associations of their lives, the scenes rendered classic in their traditions, we will not dole out to them a miser's pittance in

return for what they know to be a princely realm.

Some historians have seen General Carleton's actions as beneficial and sympathetic to the Navajo; others have viewed them as a "testing ground for the reservation policy" and have charged him with "employing his wartime powers to the limit." Carleton believed he could force the Navajo to learn to farm in the white man's fashion; the younger generations to be schooled in reading, writing, and arithmetic; and all to be taught "the truths of Christianity." As the older generation passed on, he reasoned, they would take with them "all latent longings for murdering and robbing."

But that education was virtually impossible in the conditions at the Bosque Redondo. Starvation and disease took a heavy toll among the Navajo. While under his military control, Carleton was forced to put his guard troops on half rations to share food to prevent their wards from continued starvation. Even so, women, children, and old people—noncombatants all—were treated as bad as or worse than Confederate prisoners of war in the worst Yankee camps. Many Navajo died before the Indian Department returned them to their own country in 1867 and gave the tribe new flocks and herds to start the defeated people on the path to better lives.

While Kit Carson conducted a scorched-earth policy against the Navajo, another campaign resembling Sherman's march through Georgia took place in Indian Territory. Since December 1863, Col. William Phillips, with his Kansas Indian Brigade and some white troops adding up to about 1,500 cavalrymen, rode roughshod over the eastern part of the Territory, punishing the members of the Five Civilized Tribes still in rebellion.

Before launching his vengeful column, Phillips told his men: "Those who are still in arms are rebels, and ought to die. Do not kill a prisoner after he has surrendered. But I do not want you to take prisoners. I do ask you to make your footsteps severe and terrible."

During early 1864 Phillips's Indian and white horsemen marched about four hundred miles, reported 250 Confederate Indians and Texans killed, and returned to Fort Gibson without losing a single man. On their return they learned they had a new commander, Gen. James G. Blunt, at Fort Smith. Blunt arrived on the border between Arkansas and the Territory to take command under the order establishing the Department of Kansas, which specified that the department included the "military post of Fort Smith." When Blunt arrived he was furious to discover that the order had been interpreted literally, and the town of Fort Smith, around the post itself, was under control of Brig. Gen. John M. Thayer of the Department of Arkansas.

All Blunt commanded was the fort, a "stone enclosure about 200 feet square." Most of the Union troops in the area were billeted in the town around it. Blunt tried to control all the Yankee soldiers by withholding rations from his commissary unless they reported to him for orders, but demands for his removal rose all the way to Gen. Ulysses S. Grant. The commander of all Union forces ordered Blunt removed from command at Fort Smith. Blunt found himself assigned to western Kansas with only three hundred troops, parts of regiments from Wisconsin, Iowa, and Kansas, at his disposal.

Blunt was not the only problem officer from Kansas. In late summer 1863, in retaliation for Quantrill's infamous attack on Lawrence, Brig. Gen. Thomas Ewing issued the equally infamous Order No. 11 declaring the evacuation of all Missouri counties that bordered Kansas. Both Ewing and his order became an embarrassment, so in February 1864, he was assigned to command Colorado Territory. Although Ewing would use the influence of his brother-in-law, Gen. William Tecumseh Sherman, to move him from that out-of-the-way theater to more urbane St. Louis—leaving the former Kansas preacher John M. Chivington in military command—there was a need for a military presence on the plains to which Blunt and Ewing were sent.

Several parties of Indian raiders attacked wagon trains on

the Santa Fe Trail west of Fort Larned. Other raiders stole live-stock from settlers in eastern Colorado Territory. During the investigation by officers of the Fort Larned garrison of one of the Colorado raids the long-knife soldiers discovered that a family of four white settlers had been brutally killed by Plains Indian warriors. Because the Southern Cheyenne had been very active around Fort Larned and reports of their depreda-tions flooded into the infantry post, the perpetrators were assumed to be Cheyenne.

The bodies of the settler, his wife, and his children, throats cut, mutilated, and scalped, were placed on public display in Denver, the gold rush boomtown only five years old, that sum-mer of 1864. It was a clear and ghastly sign that the Plains Indians were on the warpath. And not only on the plains of Kansas and Colorado Territory, but hostilities spread from the Texas Panhandle to Dakota Territory.

Some Yankee newspaper editors accused Confederates of stirring up the wild and free Indians on the frontier. But the Indian wars on the plains during the Civil War were really the result of a clash of cultures and poor treatment by Federal offi-cials and civilians. Before the white men's war broke out, Fort Larned was garrisoned by companies of the Second U.S. Dragoons. With the war in progress, the regular army units were transferred to the East, and the post was occupied by companies of volunteers from Kansas, Colorado Territory, and Wisconsin. These units changed from time to time, but for the most part the garrison consisted of Lt. W. F. Crocker's Ninth Wisconsin Battery, Light Artillery.

Down south in Texas under-strength companies of Texas Confederates garrisoned posts like Fort Belknap and Fort Davis, but with the exception of the Comanche who were perennial enemies of anyone from Texas, the Indian wars had little effect on the plains early in 1864. Between there and Kansas, Kiowa and Comanche raided freely, undeterred by threats made by Indian agents before the war. Agent Robert Miller had threatened Kiowa leader Little Mountain in 1858 that unless the Kiowa ceased raiding, the government would send troops to punish them.

No troops or reprisals came, since the white army became occupied with the Civil War. By the trading season of 1864, when the grass greened enough for the oxen on the trails to graze, drivers of freight wagons feared for their lives and their cargoes on the plains crossings. The Denver and Santa Fe areas began running short of food. Mail service to Santa Fe stopped because of Kiowa raids on stagecoaches and stations.

In July 1864, a Kiowa leader named White Bear leading a war party ranged far and wide on the Southern Plains. They attacked a ranch near Fort Lyon, Colorado Territory. Then they killed four white men at a stagecoach station a short distance away. A few days later White Bear's Kiowa struck a small settlement far to the south near Menard, Texas, killing several settlers. Before the month was out, a different Kiowa war party viciously attacked a train of freight wagons near the Santa Fe Trail in Kansas and killed ten teamsters. Raids continued sporadically during the rest of the summer. Then in October, Kiowa and some Comanche went on a rampage along Elm Creek near Fort Belknap, Texas. Eleven people were killed, and seven were taken hostage.

North of Kansas, Santee Sioux refugees had fled Minnesota and crossed the Missouri River into Dakota Territory. They joined other Sioux—Hunkpapa, Brule, Sans Arc, Miniconjou, and Blackfeet—and shared their plight. The Plains Sioux were incited, again not by Rebels but instead by the treatment of fellow Indians, fleeing the wrath of Minnesotans.

That summer, gold in Montana and Idaho Territories drew a new influx of fortune seekers, some of them deserters from both the Union and Confederate armies, further aggravating the Sioux and Northern Cheyenne across whose countries the gold rushers raced. The year before, Henry H. Sibley and Brig. Gen. Alfred Sully campaigned against the Santee and the Plains Sioux in eastern Dakota Territory, and Gen. Patrick Edward Connor marched from Camp Butler at Salt Lake City

*Santee Sioux fled to their kinsmen on the plains
after the Minnesota uprising.*

to harass the Sioux along the central Oregon Trail and its cut-off to California.

Gen. John Pope, still smarting at his dismissal to Minnesota after his poor showing as leader of the Army of the Potomac, formulated a plan for ending the difficulties with the Sioux. He built a force of available men, commanded by General Sully, and sent them into the field to engage the Sioux in battle. Sully was also responsible for establishing strong posts in Dakota Territory. These forts were a response to the demands for protection by gold rushers heading toward the Rockies and by settlers claiming cheap land under the Homestead Act.

Raids and killings by Sioux heightened the whites' fear of the proud warriors. Sully set out with about 1,800 troops from Nebraska and Iowa regiments to establish the forts expected of him to protect the northern overland routes and the Missouri River route west. During the march, some Sioux warriors killed the mixed brigade's topographical engineer. The cavalrymen killed three of the Sioux. As a warning, Sully ordered their heads hoisted on poles. Instead of being warned, the Sioux were infuriated; their determination to oppose the army increased.

Minnesota troops rendezvoused on June 30 with Sully's force at the mouth of Burdache Creek on the Upper Missouri for active campaigning. The combined columns numbered about 2,500 men. They established Fort Rice on July 7 at the mouth of the Cannonball River, then moved deeper into Sioux country escorting an emigrant train to the mouth of the Yellowstone River in Montana Territory. The Sioux, who had been active north of that area, moved across the Missouri and gathered a large body of warriors in an encampment on a strong position on the Little Missouri River, about two hundred miles from Fort Rice.

Sully left the emigrants with a guard and rode out in 110-degree heat toward the Killdeer Mountains with 2,200 soldiers to attack the large Sioux camp. There were about 1,600 warriors, including a remarkable medicine man and leader, Sitting

Bull. However, Sully reported between five and six thousand warriors "strongly posted in wooded country, very much cut up with high, rugged hills, and deep, impassable ravines." On July 28, 1864, Sully met with some of the Sioux leaders, but his attitude was haughty, and the meeting was useless. Sully then attacked.

He formed his troops into a mile-long square, with their horses, vehicles, and artillery pieces in the center. Skirmishers advanced, and there were charges and counter-charges by both sides. The fighting continued and was a draw until the howitzers were unlimbered and the combination of artillery fire and long-range sharpshooters forced the Sioux to back off. Then a charge by the Minnesota cavalry drove the Indians into the woods and ravines. The retirement turned into a running fight after the artillerymen shelled the Sioux in the timber and ravines. The Indians had to abandon their village, the food they had been preparing for winter, and most of their possessions. According to one account about 400,000 pounds of pemmican, a mixture of dried buffalo meat and berries pounded together, were left behind for Sully's men to capture. The Minnesota cavalry broke off their pursuit the next morning as the Sioux disappeared into the Dakota badlands of the Little Missouri River.

Sully and his men escorted the emigrants through the badlands and out of the Dakota Territory. Some historians think the Battle of Killdeer Mountain broke the back of Sioux resistance; others point out the harassment of the train of gold seekers and their soldier escorts as reminders that the Sioux were far from defeated. Sully met some of the remnants of the Sioux warriors that had escaped Killdeer Mountain in August 1864, and defeated them, but most of them had scattered to stock up as much for the winter as they could in the time remaining.

At the same time Gen. Robert B. Mitchell, hero commander of the Second Kansas Volunteers at Wilson's Creek, was sent to quell the Indian war in Nebraska Territory, especially along the Platte River Road. He and some Iowa volunteer troops pro-

Plains Indians cooking.

vided protection for stagecoaches and freight wagons bound for Denver and Salt Lake. Mitchell had at his disposal parts of several Iowa regiments including a young officer, Eugene F. Ware, also a Wilson's Creek veteran who would later write a firsthand account of the Nebraska campaign called *The Indian War of 1864.*

There had been clashes along the Smoky Hill Trail as the Cheyenne and Arapaho stepped up the ferocity of their resistance. Along this route and the Santa Fe Trail, new forts were established for military protection of travelers and settlers. A company of Iowa cavalry commanded by a young lieutenant named Ellsworth founded Fort Ellsworth on the Smoky Hill River about sixty miles west of Fort Riley, Kansas.

Fort Zarah was created on the Great Bend of the Arkansas River to protect the Santa Fe Trail. Fort Zarah was named for the son of Gen. Samuel Curtis, who had been with Gen. James G. Blunt's small force which had been caught in a surprise attack by Quantrill's Missouri guerrillas at Baxter Springs, Kansas, in October 1863. Companies from Wisconsin, Iowa, Colorado Territory, and the Eleventh Kansas Cavalry were assigned to these new forts and patrolled vast areas of the High Plains tracking down alleged Plains Indian raiders.

Throughout the summer the distracted white men were harassed by the plains tribes. The frontier blazed with raids designed to avenge the intrusions perceived by the Plains Indians—wagon trains, stagecoaches, telegraph poles and lines, and the stations along numerous trails that supported them. So settlements that supported trading posts, road ranches, stage stations, and telegraph huts were subject to attack by the warriors as well as the vehicles and lines of communication.

These lines of communication across the plains were important. New territories were being created, and existing states required administration and contact with the Federal government. Riches from mines in Arizona, Colorado, Montana, and Idaho territories were needed to pay for the war effort. In the summer of 1864, it was in no way clear that the war was nearing a finish. As summer turned to autumn, a last gasp of the Confederacy caused renewed concern among citizens of the Trans-Mississippi West. Rebel Gen. Sterling Price led two divisions of Missourians and a division of Arkansas recruits in an invasion of Missouri. During the time that Price's Rebel army raided through Missouri and Kansas, the defense of the frontier was virtually abandoned as troops were hastily gathered to defend against Price's invasion.

Until Price turned toward the Kansas border, Gen. Samuel Curtis, now in charge of the Department of Kansas, was chiefly concerned with the situation with the Cheyenne and Arapaho, the Comanche and Kiowa at the Santa Fe Trail. Curtis promptly summoned all his available troops. Some of his men were chasing Indians on the frontier. They met up with Gen. James G. Blunt and hastened to the Kansas-Missouri border. Curtis urged Kansas Gov. Thomas Carney to call out the state militia to supplement the five Kansas regiments available on the border.

The lack of troops was always a serious problem on the Civil War Indian frontier, but it grew extremely acute in the summer and fall of 1864. The Union turned to extreme measures to come up with additional manpower. One of the most unique attempts was the organization of the First U.S. Volunteer regiment. The First U.S. Volunteers were recruited from among prisoner of war camps holding Confederates who had surrendered. The Union officers who enlisted troops from among the prisoners argued that they would be used chiefly against Indians on the frontier instead of their former comrades in arms. They were called "Galvanized Yankees."

Although the organization of the Galvanized Yankees was no military secret—indeed, some important higher-ups, including Gen. Ulysses S. Grant, were quite opposed to it—those responsible for recruiting never issued any press releases. The first notice of their existence appeared about the same time that Price's advance toward Missouri hit the papers. At the end of August 1864, a few newspapers carried the story: "[T]he 1st

U.S. Volunteers, one thousand strong, passed over the New York Central Railroad *en route* for the West. . . . The train which carried the regiment numbered 29 cars." The report was mistaken when it claimed this first deployment of Galvanized Yankees would be against hostile Indians on the Overland Stage route in Nebraska Territory. The first regiment was employed in Minnesota and the Missouri River forts.

Many of the Galvanized Yankees were recruited at Camp Douglas in Illinois. Others came from the prisoner camps in Indiana, Ohio, and New York. Six regiments, nearly 6,000 former rebels, enlisted with the understanding that they would not be expected to fight against Confederates. Some enlisted to escape the horrors of prisoner of war camps. Some joined up planning to desert at the first opportunity. Secretary of War Stanton and the proponents of enlisting prisoners were in a minority—more on both the Union and Confederate fronts strongly objected to releasing prisoners of war to serve against Indians.

As the war against white men was prosecuted vigorously, and as the frontier was further drained of white soldiers, the High Plains flamed long after the usual season for warfare among the Plains Indians had passed. The plains tribes discovered that more white soldiers had suddenly become available. To begin, the defeat of the Navajo early in 1864 freed Kit Carson and the First New Mexico Volunteers for service east of their home territory.

The Comanche and Kiowa raiders were under the impression that they were secure from white vengeance. In the fall of 1864, Carson was ordered by General Carleton to launch a punitive campaign against the plains tribes like the one he had conducted that spring against the Navajo.

By November, most of the Kiowa and Comanche were in their winter camps, with their marauding suspended as their ponies, subsisting on the dried, sparse winter grass and cottonwood bark, were unfit for war parties. Carson led his regiment of fourteen officers, more than three hundred troopers, and about seventy Ute and Jicarilla Apache scouts out of Cimarron, New Mexico Territory. Totally unsuspecting, Little Mountain's Kiowa were camped with some Comanche on the Canadian River in the Texas Panhandle.

Carson's mounted troops attacked on the bitterly cold morning of November 26, Little Mountain's people reacted quickly in spite of the surprise. The Kiowa leader promptly organized warriors in an orderly retreat, protecting noncombatants while sending a rider with a plea for help to other Kiowa and Comanche encampments up and down the Canadian. Little Mountain directed the defense from horseback until his pony was shot from beneath him. He clambered to his feet and rallied his braves until reinforcements arrived from the other camps.

Suddenly, Kit Carson found himself on the defensive. The battle raged up and down the valley. Carson's column was stretched over the river bottoms and surrounding hills, with almost thirty vehicles and infantry scattered, desperate to defend themselves from the growing number of Comanche reinforcements. Carson pushed on to Adobe Walls, a fortified, Spanish-style trading post built by William Bent some two decades earlier.

The New Mexican veteran soldiers might well have been overwhelmed if not for a pair of 12-pounder mountain howitzers commanded by Lt. George H. Pettis. The young officer had the big guns loaded with exploding shells to break up concentrations of Kiowa. Little Mountain, ably helped by Stumbling Bear, Iron Shirt, and Satanta, completely circled his forces around Carson's position. To maintain contact with his scattered forces the soldiers used bugles, but it is said that Satanta, who had acquired a bugle of his own during his raiding, sounded bugle calls back to Carson's men until the soldiers were utterly confused.

The Kiowa reentered the camp they had fled in the morning. Because the wagons had not yet caught up to the attacking columns, the soldiers' ammunition ran low by the afternoon. Carson withdrew his troops to protect the lines

*William Bent was married to two Cheyenne women
and had sons who rode with the hostiles.*

Adobe Walls.

back to the supply train. Kiowa warriors tried to block the withdrawal by setting a prairie fire between the troops and the river, but Carson ordered backfires and withdrew to a commanding knoll where the howitzers continued to disconcert the Kiowa. The Indians finally pulled back, taking their pony herd with them, but the soldiers came back into the village where they burned 176 tepees, along with all the buffalo robes, winter provisions, and clothing stored in them. Iron Shirt died when he refused to abandon his lodge.

Concerned with the continuing sporadic attacks and realizing that there were literally thousands of Kiowa and Comanche in the valley, Carson ordered a retreat. The united parts of his command camped overnight, and on the morning of November 27 the celebrated mountain man led a general withdrawal from Texas, having been fought to a draw. According to the official report, the First New Mexico and Indian scouts lost three killed and twenty-five wounded, three of them fatally. According to Carson's account, the Indians lost sixty killed and 150 wounded. One Comanche scalp was reportedly taken by a young Mexican recruit among the soldiers.

After nearly two years of campaigning, the First New Mexico regiment disbanded upon its return to Fort Bascom. General Carleton praised Colonel Carson's retreat in good order, when in fact the Kiowa allowed him to escape because they were stunned by his unexpected blow. Carleton claimed a decisive victory, but Carson later admitted that if Adobe Walls was to become a military post at least 1,000 troops fully equipped and artillery would be necessary to maintain order among the tribes of the Southern Plains.

The same week Carson's men fought Kiowa and Comanche at Adobe Walls, another surprise attack a few hundred miles north had decidedly different results.

Black Kettle had been a noted warrior in his youth; he was a noted leader of the Southern Cheyenne in his middle age. In 1863, he had been to the important white city of Washington, had shaken the hand of Great Father Lincoln, and had been

Plains Indian warrior's funeral platform after the battle at Adobe Walls.

gifted a thirty-four-star American flag from the Commissioner of Indian Affairs. He was told that bluecoat soldiers would never attack anyone protected by this flag. Once back on the plains, Black Kettle flew that flag constantly above his lodge in the middle of his encampment. He had declared himself and his band for peace, and he thought the whites understood that he did not control the Cheyenne Dog Soldiers.

Despite his best efforts and the military protection of Fort Lyon, indiscriminate attacks by both sides increased in intensity during the fall of 1864. The territorial governor of Colorado, John Evans, ordered all friendly Indians to report to the nearest local fort where they could be protected. The officials at Fort Lyon told Black Kettle to camp on Sand Creek on the eastern plains of Colorado Territory.

By the autumn of 1864, Sioux, Southern Cheyenne, and Arapaho were in control of all lines of communication east of Denver. Colorado mail was detoured via the Isthmus of Panama and California, some of it on the old Pony Express route. The price of goods, already high because Denver was a gold rush boomtown, soared astronomically. Governor Evans and his cronies considered Denver besieged, confirmed by the display of the settler and his family who had been slaughtered in the town's near vicinity. Every able-bodied man, whether pro-Southern or Unionist, was enrolled in the military, armed and drilled.

Appeals were made for Colorado troops to be returned from the Union armies, but those regiments were employed in fending off Price's raid into Kansas. A call was made for assistance from some of Carleton's troops in New Mexico and Arizona Territories, but of course, those available were already campaigning with Kit Carson punishing the tribes of the Southern Plains in the Texas Panhandle. The hue and cry caused by the public display of the settler family was what Governor Evans needed to convince Washington to allow the creation of a regiment of Indian fighters.

The Third Colorado Volunteer Cavalry regiment was raised

Southern Cheyenne set up camp at Sand Creek.

strictly for that purpose. The enlistees in the unit were hundred-day volunteers. The governor assured them that they would not depart the territory but would only fight poorly armed Indians instead of seasoned Confederate veterans as the other two Colorado regiments were doing. As Evans explained, "They have been raised to kill Indians, and they must kill Indians." He revealed both his prejudice and his commitment to a political course of action.

In military command of the volunteers was Col. John M. Chivington. He had been a Methodist Episcopal minister in Kansas and a missionary to Indians. After moving to Denver he became politically connected and espoused the militarism of the era. He was a hero of Glorietta Pass against Rebels, and now he and his men were primed to impose a terrible punishment on peace-seeking Indians. Chivington himself echoed Governor Evans' sentiments when asked later about the extermination policy, which included children as well as adults: "Nits make lice."

With the blessing of higher authorities including Evans, General Carleton, and General Connor, Chivington organized a campaign late in the year but before his hundred-day soldiers' recruitments expired. In November 1864, he marched from a camp near Denver with 750 cavalrymen, two-thirds of whom were new recruits, and several field pieces. At sunrise on November 29, 1864—just three days after Kit Carson's surprise attack on the Kiowa village—the Third Colorado fell upon the combined villages of Black Kettle and the Arapaho chief White Antelope. There was about the same number of Cheyenne and Arapaho in the Sand Creek village. Two-thirds of them were noncombatants—women, children, old people, and peaceful warriors. Black Kettle pointed out the Stars and Stripes and a smaller white flag in the freezing morning sun. He told his people gathered around him not to fear, and called the attention of the soldiers to the flags on his lodge pole at the center of the camp.

No scraps of cloth could save them. Chivington ordered a

Black Kettle's flags in the Sand Creek village.

three-armed assault, one column swinging out to cut off the horse herd while the other two surrounded Black Kettle's camp of about 130 lodges. Rifle fire crackled, musket balls cut through the air, and the field pieces boomed gutturally, belching explosive shells. Some of the Cheyenne and Arapaho escaped by slipping up the creek bed, while others mounted a determined defense for almost two hours. Then the guns were brought into play to scatter and rout the Indians. A five-mile running fight ensured until dusk. Two women and five youngsters were all that were captured. Estimates of Indian deaths range from a conservative hundred women and children and twenty-eight men to more than three hundred killed, half of them warriors. Casualties among the Coloradans amounted to seven killed, forty-seven wounded—seven of the latter died later.

Chivington was initially acclaimed as a hero, then castigated for the bloody vengeance. Two weeks after Sand Creek, he was honored with a parade down the main street of Denver. He appeared on stage at the opera house displaying some of the revolting trophies. A Denver newspaper opined: "Among the brilliant feats of arms in Indian warfare, the recent campaign of our Colorado volunteers will stand in history with few rivals, and none to exceed it in final results." Then it added: "Colorado soldiers have again covered themselves with glory."

But opinion changed. The feeling was that the attack at Sand Creek was justified but not its manner nor its violence. An investigation was conducted, and Chivington was ordered to face a court-martial. He was mustered out before the court could be convened. "To the abstract question," wrote one Coloradan, "whether it is right to kill women and children, there can be but one answer. But as a matter of retaliation, and a matter of policy, whether those people were right in killing women and children at Sand Creek is a question to which the answer does not come so glibly."

Meanwhile, the Southern Cheyenne survivors—about eighty-five men and ninety-five women and children—escaped to a breathtaking array of deep canyons, an anomaly of the High Plains, stretching across the corners of Kansas and Nebraska Territory. The rugged terrain had been sculpted by wind and water in the deep layers of loess deposited there, known as the Arikaree Breaks, between the Smoky Hill Trail and the Platte River Road southeast of Julesburg, Colorado Territory. West of Julesburg was a road ranch reminiscent of a medieval castle—thick sod and adobe brick walls surrounded by a moat, and an outer wall of stone. Above the gate was a crude hand-lettered sign proclaiming it was "Fort Wicked, Kept by W. Godfrey." When asked why he called it Fort Wicked, Mr. Godfrey replied that the Sioux and Cheyenne knew well enough—he and his post had survived several strong attacks during the Indian war along the Platte. Black Kettle's survivors came to the Arikaree Breaks to regroup and recover.

As news of the tragic and vengeful massacre spread across the plains, hundreds of Sioux, Cheyenne, Arapaho, and other tribes joined the handful of survivors in the breaks to plot their revenge. Surrounded by abundant yucca, sage, and native buffalo grass, the deep arroyos of the breaks hid the large gathering of warriors from white knowledge. These Indians would strike back at the very beginning of the next year.

Canyon de Chelly, Killdeer Mountain, Adobe Walls, Sand Creek, and many smaller massacres of Indians stand as somber pages in the chronicle of total warfare unfolding across America in 1864. As Grant threw thousands of Union soldiers into the meat grinder of the Wilderness, as Sherman marched through Georgia leaving a smoking path of destruction, so Kit Carson, Alfred Sully, and John M. Chivington waged total war on the Indians on the frontier. The war between the whites was now drawing to a close—the war between Indians and whites just took a sharp turn toward increased violence.

Col. Thomas Moonlight.

CHAPTER 5

"Boots and Saddles": 1865

Wars between the United States and foreign powers had often presented Indians with what seemed to them opportunities to reclaim some of their lost homelands or at least to hold their hunting grounds for a time. But never was their chance so good as when the American people were distracted and the soldiers withdrawn from the West as the nation split against itself. For four years the Civil War had been a conflict that slowed the threat to the existence of the tribes while it threatened the very existence of the nation itself. In early 1865, hope and hatred revived in thousands of lodges across the plains. As early as January that year there was a renewal of savage attacks on settlements and overland stations. Cheyenne, Arapaho, and Sioux congregated in northwestern Kansas after the Sand Creek massacre.

Called the Cherry Creek encampment, the Southern Cheyenne survivors were joined by hundreds of Sioux and Cheyenne until the Arikaree Breaks seemed filled with tepees and swarmed with angry men infuriated by the brutal bloodbath at Sand Creek. Even before Chivington's Third Colorado regiment could celebrate their dubious victory, Indians planned to strike back violently against the whites. They chose as their target a key town on the Republican River Road—Julesburg, in northeastern Colorado Territory.

On New Year's Day 1865, a great war party of Cheyenne, Sioux, and Arapaho struck out from the Breaks and passed through Devil's Gap, some astoundingly deep canyons winding out of the rugged country, on their way to attack Julesburg. On the night of January 6 they camped near the important point on Ben Holliday's Overland Stage route. Not far away was a post called Fort Rankin, occupied by a company of the Seventh Iowa Volunteer Cavalry regiment. Not long after dawn a half-dozen warriors led by Big Crow, a noted Cheyenne, rode out of an arroyo near the post to attack some civilian employees working outside the defenses.

The white men dashed inside, and the Iowa cavalry hastened to answer the "Boots and Saddles" bugle call to give chase to the audacious Indians. At top speed soldiers goaded their horses in pursuit of the seven warriors toward the sand hills a couple of miles away. The Iowans' leader, a Captain O'Brien, sought to capture the hostiles before they reached the hills, but it seemed that Big Crow's party always managed to stay just out of reach. Then, as the cavalrymen neared the sand hills, the crest of a ridge seemed to sprout a war party of incredible size.

It was an old trick, but it would be used successfully time after time during the Indian wars of the late nineteenth century. The seven warriors were decoys, luring the Iowa cavalrymen into a deadly trap. It quickly became a fight for life. Captain O'Brien and his command hightailed it back to Fort Rankin in a desperate ride for safety—but not all of the whites made it. A sergeant, fourteen enlisted men, and four civilians died in the running fight.

When the white men had taken cover inside the post, the Sioux and Cheyenne circled the stockade, filling the air with war cries and feathered shafts. The population of Julesburg had taken refuge in Fort Rankin, but with no one in town the Indians were free to plunder the empty buildings. They returned through Devil's Gap to the Cherry Creek encampment in the Arikaree Breaks. There they shared the booty from Julesburg.

Three weeks later the warriors struck out again. On January 28, 1865, they attacked Harlow's Ranch on the Overland Stage line, burning it, killing two employees, and carrying off a female victim. The same day, Indians raided three other places on the Platte River Road. Buildings and haystacks were burned, stores and warehouses were looted, and a paralyzing campaign against the stage and freight route ensured for weeks.

On that January 28 raid, the Cheyenne got some signal revenge when nine recently discharged men from the Third Colorado—men who had taken part in the Sand Creek massacre—were caught by a band of warriors. The former hundred-day volunteers were on their way to the East, but the Cheyenne killed all of them. When the white men's belongings were looted, two Cheyenne scalps from Sand Creek were recognized by the captors because of their hair ornaments. They were infuriated all over again, and they literally cut the dead bodies into pieces.

During the first two weeks of February 1865, the allied Plains Indian tribes attacked and burned seven road ranches along the Platte River Road. At the last one, seven white men were killed and the owner's wife and child carried into captivity. Three freighters' wagon trains were captured and ransacked. In a second raid on Julesburg, there was virtually no resistance offered, so the town was harried by Indians while soldiers watched helplessly from Fort Rankin only a mile distant. Scores of white people, both civilians and those men in the service, paid the ultimate price for the Sand Creek debacle. The Southern Cheyenne became the most dangerous adversaries of the Union west of the Missouri River in the first half of 1865.

The spring of 1865 brought another event, far to the east, which involved an American Indian. The man was Ely Parker, the Seneca sachem, Ulysses S. Grant's military secretary, and a lieutenant colonel in the Union Army. In April 1865, Parker drafted the two copies of the document by which Gen. Robert E. Lee surrendered his Army of Northern Virginia. Parker's

Seneca forebears had succumbed to a proud but sure conquest just like the defeat of the once mighty Rebel army Parker now witnessed. One of the tables on which the surrender documents were signed by Lee and Grant was gifted to the new wife of a future famous Indian fighter. She was Elizabeth Bacon Custer, married in 1864 to Maj. Gen. George Armstrong Custer, who less than a dozen years later died fighting against Sioux and Cheyenne on the Little Bighorn River in Montana.

The raiding on the plains continued through the spring and early summer of 1865. In July, the Cheyenne and Sioux appeared near the Platte River Bridge Station where a small stockade was garrisoned by some of the Eleventh Kansas Volunteer Cavalry. The Eleventh Kansas was commanded by Col. Thomas Moonlight, a self-made Scot who came across the Atlantic as a boy, served in the regular army artillery, and retired to a farm near Fort Leavenworth. When the war erupted, Moonlight enlisted and was eventually promoted to command his own regiment. Under him, the Eleventh Kansas became one of the best fighting units on the Kansas-Missouri border. The men of the regiment took part in a fighting withdrawal in front of Sterling Price's army before fighting at the Battle of Westport, Missouri. Before any of the Kansans had time to relax, nine companies of their regiment were ordered to Fort Kearny, Nebraska Territory. The troopers marched from Kansas City to Fort Riley along the Kansas River road, then north along the Republican River road. At Fort Kearny, the Eleventh Kansas was piecemealed out in companies at lonesome posts along the Platte River Road to patrol and protect freighters and stagecoach drivers and passengers. The Platte River Bridge Station was one of those posts where the trail crossed the river via a crude bridge.

As the war between the white men drew to a writhing close, the Sioux and Cheyenne harassed and scouted the Platte River Road with its Overland Mail and Pacific Telegraph lines and Holliday's stagecoach route. In spite of the small size, the combined tribes recognized the threat it posed to their land, their people, and their way of life. Indian scouts reported more bluecoat soldiers along the trail. Some of these were seven companies of the Eleventh Kansas. Some were part of Col. Samuel Walker's Sixteenth Kansas Volunteer Cavalry regiment. And some were Galvanized Yankees.

No fanfare accompanied the creation of six regiments—between 5,000 and 6,000 men—of Confederate prisoners of war late in 1864. But the first months of 1865, the First, Second, and Third U.S. Volunteer Infantry regiments had been deployed. The First was merely on garrison duty, but the Second regiment was along the Santa Fe Trail, relatively peaceful after Colonel Carson's fight at Adobe Walls, and the Third was headquartered at busy Fort Kearny, joining the Kansas state volunteers patrolling the Platte.

The Santa Fe Trail was relatively peaceful because a remarkable Kiowa leader, Satanta, had gone south. He had constantly lurked within a few miles of Pawnee Rock, a promontory in south central Kansas on the trail. From there he had led a combined force of Kiowa and Comanche sweeping down on thinly protected mail coaches and teams of freight wagons, loaded going southwest, nearly empty returning to the northeast. Satanta's Kiowa and Comanche had virtually closed the Santa Fe Trail early in the Civil War. Their constant raiding was at least partly responsible for the attack by Chivington and the Third Colorado at Sand Creek. After Carson's Adobe Walls fight, Satanta and his followers went to ground for the rest of the winter. That 1865 summer he led his band deep into Texas and Mexico far from the reach of long knives and bluecoat soldiers. He wanted to return in the fall for the Little Arkansas treaty powwow, but a couple years later he joined the Southern Cheyenne on the warpath.

The leaders of the combined tribes opposing the Galvanized Yankees, the Eleventh Kansas contingent, and the other state volunteers were Red Cloud of the Sioux and Roman Nose of the Southern Cheyenne. Red Cloud was certainly one of the most capable leaders of the Plains Indians in the nineteenth

Red Cloud, leader of the Sioux, in American attire.

century, implacable in war, tactful and diplomatic in peace. Roman Nose was not only wily but, because he believed himself invulnerable in battle, was also a fearless example to his vengeful Cheyenne. As warm weather approached, Roman Nose and Red Cloud decided to hit the soldiers at a point where they were most distant from any help. The weakest link in the chain of defense along the road was the Platte River Bridge Station, guarded by Kansans and Galvanized Yankees in the vicinity.

The Eleventh Kansas took up their post at Platte River Bridge in early May 1865—a month after Robert E. Lee had surrendered at Appomattox and while Joseph Johnston was surrendering to General Sherman in the Carolinas. In June 1865, the last regiment of Galvanized Yankees to be organized marched to the Platte River Road from Fort Leavenworth. The Sixth U.S. Volunteers replaced the Third U.S. Volunteers out of Fort Kearny. By the time they arrived, the Cheyenne and Sioux were putting pressure on the Eleventh Kansas and the scattered units of other regiments in the vicinity.

Indeed, the white soldiers had their hands full throughout much of the Northern Plains. Trying to patrol and control what amounted to most of the Missouri River drainage system kept troops busy from Denver to Fort Riley in central Kansas and from there to the Dakotas.

At Fort Rice, Sioux warriors inspired by soon to be legendary leader Sitting Bull attacked dismounted soldiers under Lt. Col. John Pattee of the Galvanized Yankees; only discipline, courage, a pair of swivel howitzers, and two 12-pounders on the fort's parade ground turned back the superb horsemen of the Plains. In a three-hour battle, the warriors charged, peppering their enemy with arrows, but the surprise firepower often made all the difference. Of two companies of the Fourth U.S. Volunteers, the Galvanized Yankees, and a company of the Seventh Iowa Volunteer Cavalry, one soldier was killed and another was mortally wounded. While the fighting was still in progress, the Sioux removed their casualties from the field.

The Eleventh Kansas at the Platte River Bridge.

Indians cut telegraph lines at the Platte River Bridge.

In June and July 1865, Gen. Patrick Edward Connor was preoccupied with organizing his expedition to the Powder River country of Montana Territory where a road was to be built to the new gold fields opened the year before. Connor seemed, according to some historians, to feel that many of the Indian troubles plaguing the Overland Mail Route would be served best by his thrust at the villages on the Platte River. As he prepared for the campaign, Connor collected all available mounted troops. He was anxious to put his own California cavalry to good use. They were at Fort Douglas near Salt Lake. After long consideration, Connor ordered the mounted Californians from Utah Territory to the Powder River, replacing them with Galvanized Yankees of the Sixth U.S. Volunteers. The Civil War would be completely over, in the sense that the last organized Confederate armies had surrendered, before Connor's force of Californians, Galvanized Yankees, and assorted other companies set out to punish Sioux and Cheyenne in Montana country.

Along the Platte River Road, Col. Thomas Moonlight decided to lead an armed reconnaissance of elements of his Eleventh Kansas in the direction of Fort Mitchell, some miles north of the Platte Bridge. Moonlight assumed command of the area from the disgraced Colonel Chivington after the whole Sand Creek affair. Moonlight presided at the court-martial of the Colorado colonel. He also had to contend with Col. Sam Walker's Sixteenth Kansas Volunteers who had enlisted for three years or until the war ended, whichever came first. Since Lee's surrender at Appomattox, the troopers of the Sixteenth Kansas considered the war over and wanted to go home immediately. Some in the regiment were virtually mutinous by June 1865, even though there were still Confederate armies in the field that had not yet surrendered. Obviously, none of these were in the Denver vicinity where some of the regiment served, but there were plenty of Sioux.

The Sioux permitted Moonlight to lead his reconnaissance group toward Fort Mitchell, and to exhaust more than half of his force of 350 men and horses, including elements of two regiments of Californians, one of Ohioans, and the Eleventh and the Sixteenth Kansas regiments. After the force was reduced to about 135 men, the Cheyenne and Sioux ambushed the force during a noon halt. Moonlight and his mixed bag were forced to beat an ignominious retreat on foot, after suffering several casualties and losing more than half of their remaining horses. Moonlight and his command reached Fort Halleck on June 20, 1865, and were joined by two additional companies of the Eleventh Kansas on June 26.

The troops of the region were scattered in small contingents miles apart from each other. Roman Nose saw that the largest force remained at the Platte River Bridge Station, and realized that once it was reduced he could eliminate the others at his leisure. The forces at the station were commanded by Maj. Martin Anderson and included parts of five companies of the Eleventh Kansas, part of a company of Galvanized Yankees, a single howitzer, and Lt. Casper Collins of the Eleventh Ohio who had come up with the mail ambulance. On July 25, a Lieutenant Bretnay of the Eleventh Ohio also arrived from the East with a few men of his company and reported that they had passed a wagon train protected by troops under a Sergeant Custard.

Major Anderson ordered up a twenty-five-man detail to warn and assist Sergeant Custard at Willow Spring. Roman Nose's Cheyenne tried springing the same trap that Sitting Bull's Sioux had used against Colonel Pattee's Galvanized Yankees at Fort Rice on July 28, 1865. At the Platte River Bridge, the twenty-five troopers raced back to the relative safety of the post. The soldiers at the station dared not fire their carbines or the howitzer for fear of injuring their retreating comrades.

At first Lieutenant Collins tried to fight his way forward, but as the number of Cheyenne steadily grew he ordered his patrol to fall back. By then the Cheyenne had blocked his way to the bridge. Collins's head was pierced by an arrow, but according to George Bent who was with the Cheyenne that day, the lieutenant's horse ran away with him after the arrow wound. Other writers say he kept leading the retreat until he was dragged from his mount. He and many of his little command were killed. Only a remnant won their way through to the bridge.

In the meantime, Sergeant Custard's escort and the wagon train were attacked. Five men had ridden ahead when the column heard the howitzer of the fort—only three made it through to the bridge. Custard circled his wagons. His escort and the wagons' teamsters opened up with carbines as Cheyenne on horseback swarmed around them. A few dropped from their horses, and they drew out of range.

Then Roman Nose personally took the field. He rode slowly around the beleaguered wagon corral. He then had his Cheyenne dismount, and every one of them with a gun crept as close to the enclosure as possible. Even though Plains Indians were not remarkable as marksmen, the withering fire had the desired effect. About midafternoon, Roman Nose ceased the firing and rode again alone around the wagons to draw fire. When no shots sounded, he entered the circle. Those whites who were not dead were seriously wounded. The dead were the fortunate ones as the Cheyenne took more revenge for Chivington's folly.

Major Anderson and Captain Walker watched with field glasses as the wagon train was demolished. They expected the Cheyenne to turn on their stockade next. They were cut off from any help. They were surprised moments after the wagons were fired by the Cheyenne victors to see three men leading their mounts, trailed by about fifty Indians. At first it was assumed that this was another decoy to draw soldiers from their cover, but then it was realized that they were three survivors of the wagon train, so they were met by a rescue party. As night fell, the Indians drew off, having inflicted twenty-six dead and seven wounded casualties among the Eleventh Kansas.

As summer approached, Confederate forces in the Carolinas had also capitulated. Confederate Indians in the Territory remained defiant. Stand Watie had been promoted to brigadier general. He had captured Tahlequah, the Cherokee capital in

Indian Territory, and burned his rival's stately Southern mansion. Leading a raid toward the southern border of Kansas he had been turned back only by Col. William Phillips and the Union Indian Brigade. Throughout the war to its end Gen. Stand Watie's destructive raids were comparable to those of Rebel guerrilla William Clarke Quantrill, and he was the last Confederate general to surrender his command on June 23, 1865.

While the Civil War wound down and the war on the Platte blazed, the war on the Southern Plains heated up as well. Word of the treachery of whites at Sand Creek spread to the Comanche and Kiowa, who after Adobe Walls joined with Southern Cheyenne south of the Arkansas River to strike back.

On February 1, 1865, Plains Indians attacked a party of soldiers chopping wood outside Fort Zarah on the Great Bend of the Arkansas River in central Kansas. The Indian troubles on the Santa Fe Trail had caused military posts to be created and garrisoned with Wisconsin and Iowa soldiers as well as two companies of the Eleventh Kansas.

On February 11, a small squad of cavalry scouts rode out on patrol from Fort Larned, as they had done all winter. This time snow exceeded a foot deep and the temperature was below zero. Despite the attack on the Fort Zarah woodcutters, the patrol from Fort Larned reported that all was quiet on the Indian frontier in that area—they still believed the southern tribes were pacified after Adobe Walls.

Tensions on the Southern Plains mounted in spite of attempts to negotiate with Cheyenne, Kiowa, and Comanche. On April 10, 1865—the day after Lee's Palm Sunday surrender in Virginia—Fort Dodge was established at a ford of the Arkansas River west of Fort Larned. Col. James Ford of the Second Colorado Volunteers, who was transferred to the plains after helping defeat Price's Rebels at Westport, sent a short battalion under Capt. Henry Pearce and his Company C, Eleventh Kansas Volunteers, two companies of Galvanized Yankees from the Second U.S. Volunteers, and Company K of Ford's Second

Colorado, to establish a post near where the Santa Fe Trail split into two routes. The post was named Fort Dodge after Gen. Grenville M. Dodge who commanded the military district.

Even so, the Indian wars in Kansas flared throughout April. Isolated raids culminated in a major attack on April 24 when Cheyenne struck a wagon train on the Santa Fe Trail fifteen miles east of Fort Zarah. Col. James H. Leavenworth had made a march south of the Arkansas River to open talks with Arapaho and Cheyenne bands. General Dodge and Maj. Gen. Henry Halleck, commander in chief in Washington, D.C., felt that Colonel Leavenworth was making progress with his peace talks.

Halleck and Dodge ordered an expedition against the Cheyenne who had attacked the wagon train and other hostiles. Colonel Ford commanded some of his Second Colorado and some Kansas troops delayed at Fort Zarah pending Colonel Leavenworth's talks. Of course, some were anxiously waiting to be mustered out. The audacity of the wagon attack sent a clear message that the war on the plains was in earnest. Chivington's massacre was not forgotten, and the tribesmen of the Southern Plains found they could profit at the same time they wreaked vengeance.

According to frontiersman Jesse Chisholm, who maintained a trading post on the lower part of the Arkansas River in Kansas near the modern city of Wichita and made frequent trading excursions into the Nations, an Indian gathering at Fort Cobb, Indian Territory, had been addressed by a Confederate officer in the spring of 1865 with the intention of inciting the plains tribes.

Colonel Leavenworth's negotiations did not end the wars in Kansas, but they had an impact. In the fall of 1865 bands from several of the tribes of the Southern Plains would gather on the Little Arkansas River in south central Kansas to treat with white commissioners. The Little Arkansas Treaty seemed to placate the hostiles for a while, but in fact the Cheyenne and Sioux went north to carry on their warfare with Red Cloud against

Fort Phil Kearny and the Bozeman Trail. The winter of 1865 and much of 1866 were comparatively quiet in Kansas.

Throughout the rest of 1865, state volunteer regiments and companies of regiments across the West awaited orders to return home or to be mustered out. By the end of the year many of these men had rejoined their families and returned to their previous lives. The Indian wars on the plains and in the Southwest would continue for decades. But as the hostile tribesmen were forced to accept white men's control, often by the veterans of the Civil War, the western half of the United States filled with settlers, miners, farms, ranches, railroads, businesses, towns—in short, white civilization. One by one, tribes yielded to the same conquest that the Confederacy was forced to accept.

Arms went unstacked in these wars; death was as common as surrender, on both sides. Troops, a portion of the mighty armies of the Union, mustered again at the frontier forts. The Galvanized Yankees were mostly sent home in 1866, to be replaced with new cavalry regiments, including the famous Seventh U.S. Cavalry and the Ninth and Tenth U.S. Cavalry (Colored), with their Buffalo Soldiers. Veterans, and younger men, and even immigrants who carried on after them, took the field in the Indian wars. The Union generals who had had little sympathy in suppressing their fellow countrymen had no compunction in crushing the Indians.

The Indian wars fought after the Civil War would be different, more professional than those fought before the war. They would seldom be fought by militia or state volunteers but rather by regulars in an army raised to fight Indians—and that would be all that the army did until the war with Spain thirty years later. Military leaders who earlier had carried the war to the Confederacy now applied their tactics of total war to the Indians—men like Sherman, Sheridan, Custer, Grierson, Howard, Crook, Miles, and others who had fought for the Union now waged Indian wars that would ultimately change the face of the West.

*Modern travelers crossing the West are often
unaware of the significant conflicts that took place
there in earlier days.*

The conquest of Apacheria that had started with Mangas and Cochise would continue long after their demise. The conquest of the Southern Plains from Kiowa and Comanche under leaders like Satanta and Little Mountain would take years. Battles comparable in magnitude and fame to those of the Civil War would be fought before the Northern Plains were wrested from the Sioux and Northern Cheyenne. The Navajo would suffer with some Apache neighbors on the Bosque Redondo. But eventually all of Indian America would lie in the hands of the veterans of the Civil War, the men who had learned their trade fighting other white men and then turned their training, tactics, and technology on the Indians.

Today as travelers cross the American West and survey the settled, tamed landscapes along highways, experience the magnitude of large cities, and encounter the people who have populated the modern West, it is difficult to perceive the bitter conflicts that raged across the deserts and mountains, plains and prairies so long ago. Most of the sites of raids, skirmishes, and massacres have vanished with time, along with those events that affected so many of the Native Americans and the new white immigrants and settlers and the soldiers who fought some and protected others.

Still, there is practicality in recollecting the horrors of the Indian wars, the cruelty and deception and ugly, violent deaths on both sides. It helps us understand the high price paid by all for the relative prosperity of today.

To this very day the Indian wars help to define the image of the American West. The Indian wars fought during the Civil War have in many cases been forgotten. Yet they were precursors to and played integral roles in the conquest of the West, and they were as much a part of the trials and tribulations of the Civil War as the experiences in the East and in the South.

Selected Bibliography

Aleshire, Peter. *Cochise: The Life and Times of the Great Apache Chief.* New York: Wiley, 2001.

Brown, D. Alexander (Dee). *The Galvanized Yankees.* Urbana: University of Illinois Press, 1963.

Bryant, Charles S. *A History of the Great Massacre of the Sioux Indians, in Minnesota Including the Personal Narratives of Many Who Escaped.* Millwood, NY: Kraus Reprint Co., 1973.

Corley, Kenneth. *The Santee Uprising of 1862.* St Paul: Minnesota Historical Society, 1976.

Cozzens, Peter. *General John Pope: A Life for the Nation.* Urbana: University of Illinois Press, 2000.

Crawford, Samuel J. *Kansas in the Sixties.* New York: A.C. McClurg & Co., 1911.

Downey, Fairfax. *Indian Wars of the U.S. Army, 1775–1865.* New York: Doubleday, 1962.

Dunlay, Thomas W. *Kit Carson and the Indians.* Lincoln: University of Nebraska Press, 2000.

Dunn, William R. *"I Stand by Sand Creek": A Defense of Colonel John M. Chivington and the Third Colorado Cavalry.* Fort Collins: Old Army Press, 1985.

Hoig, Stan. *The Sand Creek Massacre.* Norman: University of Oklahoma Press, 1961.

Meyer, Ray Willard. *History of the Santee Sioux: United States*

Indian Policy on Trial. Lincoln: University of Nebraska Press, 1993.

Monaghan, Jay. *Civil War on the Western Border, 1854–1865.* Boston: Little, Brown and Company, 1955.

Nye, Wilbur S. *Plains Indian Raiders: The Final Phases of Warfare from the Arkansas to the Red River.* Norman: University of Oklahoma Press, 1968.

Schurz, Wallace J. *Abandoned by Lincoln: A Military Biography of General John Pope.* Urbana: University of Illinois Press, 2000.

Thrap, Dan. *The Conquest of Apacheria.* Norman: University of Oklahoma Press, 1967.

Tolzman, Don Heinrich (ed.). *The Sioux Uprising in Minnesota, 1862: Jacob Nix's Eyewitness History.* Indianapolis: Indiana University–Purdue University, 1994.

Utley, Robert M. *The Indian Frontier of the American West, 1846–1890.* Albuquerque: University of New Mexico Press, 1984.

Ware, Eugene F. *The Indian War of 1864.* New York: St. Martin's, 1960.

Wellman, Paul. *Death on the Desert and Death on the Plains.* Reprinted as one volume. New York: Curtis Books, 1969.

Index of Battles, Skirmishes, Raids, and Massacres